CS-7   GENERAL APTITUDE AND ABILITIES SERIES

This is your
PASSBOOK for...

Grammar and Usage

Test Preparation Study Guide
Questions & Answers

COPYRIGHT NOTICE

This book is SOLELY intended for, is sold ONLY to, and its use is RESTRICTED to individual, bona fide applicants or candidates who qualify by virtue of having seriously filed applications for appropriate license, certificate, professional and/or promotional advancement, higher school matriculation, scholarship, or other legitimate requirements of education and/or governmental authorities.

This book is NOT intended for use, class instruction, tutoring, training, duplication, copying, reprinting, excerption, or adaptation, etc., by:

1) Other publishers
2) Proprietors and/or Instructors of "Coaching" and/or Preparatory Courses
3) Personnel and/or Training Divisions of commercial, industrial, and governmental organizations
4) Schools, colleges, or universities and/or their departments and staffs, including teachers and other personnel
5) Testing Agencies or Bureaus
6) Study groups which seek by the purchase of a single volume to copy and/or duplicate and/or adapt this material for use by the group as a whole without having purchased individual volumes for each of the members of the group
7) Et al.

Such persons would be in violation of appropriate Federal and State statutes.

PROVISION OF LICENSING AGREEMENTS – Recognized educational, commercial, industrial, and governmental institutions and organizations, and others legitimately engaged in educational pursuits, including training, testing, and measurement activities, may address request for a licensing agreement to the copyright owners, who will determine whether, and under what conditions, including fees and charges, the materials in this book may be used them. In other words, a licensing facility exists for the legitimate use of the material in this book on other than an individual basis. However, it is asseverated and affirmed here that the material in this book CANNOT be used without the receipt of the express permission of such a licensing agreement from the Publishers. Inquiries re licensing should be addressed to the company, attention rights and permissions department.

All rights reserved, including the right of reproduction in whole or in part, in any form or by any means, electronic or mechanical, including photocopying, recording, or by any information storage and retrieval system, without permission in writing from the Publisher.

Copyright © 2024 by
National Learning Corporation

212 Michael Drive, Syosset, NY 11791
(516) 921-8888 • www.passbooks.com
E-mail: info@passbooks.com

PUBLISHED IN THE UNITED STATES OF AMERICA

PASSBOOK® SERIES

THE *PASSBOOK® SERIES* has been created to prepare applicants and candidates for the ultimate academic battlefield – the examination room.

At some time in our lives, each and every one of us may be required to take an examination – for validation, matriculation, admission, qualification, registration, certification, or licensure.

Based on the assumption that every applicant or candidate has met the basic formal educational standards, has taken the required number of courses, and read the necessary texts, the *PASSBOOK® SERIES* furnishes the one special preparation which may assure passing with confidence, instead of failing with insecurity. Examination questions – together with answers – are furnished as the basic vehicle for study so that the mysteries of the examination and its compounding difficulties may be eliminated or diminished by a sure method.

This book is meant to help you pass your examination provided that you qualify and are serious in your objective.

The entire field is reviewed through the huge store of content information which is succinctly presented through a provocative and challenging approach – the question-and-answer method.

A climate of success is established by furnishing the correct answers at the end of each test.

You soon learn to recognize types of questions, forms of questions, and patterns of questioning. You may even begin to anticipate expected outcomes.

You perceive that many questions are repeated or adapted so that you can gain acute insights, which may enable you to score many sure points.

You learn how to confront new questions, or types of questions, and to attack them confidently and work out the correct answers.

You note objectives and emphases, and recognize pitfalls and dangers, so that you may make positive educational adjustments.

Moreover, you are kept fully informed in relation to new concepts, methods, practices, and directions in the field.

You discover that you are actually taking the examination all the time: you are preparing for the examination by "taking" an examination, not by reading extraneous and/or supererogatory textbooks.

In short, this PASSBOOK®, used directedly, should be an important factor in helping you to pass your test.

SAMPLE QUESTIONS

TEST 1

ENGLISH USAGE

DIRECTIONS: Many jobs require an employee to communicate, verbally and/or in writing, in accordance with the principles of correct English usage. The questions on this test measure these abilities by testing your knowledge of grammar, punctuation, and sentence structure. In the following questions, choose the sentence that represents the BEST English usage. *PRINT THE LETTER OF THE CORRECT ANSWER IN THE SPACE AT THE RIGHT.*

1. A. Of the two runners, John is the worst.   1.____
   B. Of the two runner, John is the better.
   C. John is the worst of the two runners.
   D. John is the best of the two runners.

2. A. We seldom ever receive this type of request anymore.   2.____
   B. Neither of the employees are doing what is expected of him.
   C. Each of these regulations apply to your case.
   D. I have enclosed a copy of the file you requested.

KEY (CORRECT ANSWERS)

1. The correct answer is B. The correct way to write Option A is "Of the two runners, John is worse." The correct way to write Option C is "John is the worse of the two runners." The correct way to write Option D is "John is the better of the two runners."

2. The correct answer is D. The correct way to write Option A is "We seldom receive this type of request." The correct way to write Option B is "Neither of the employees is doing what is expected of him." The correct way to write Option C is "Each of these regulations applies to your case."

TEST 2

FOLLOWING DIRECTIONS

DIRECTIONS: The ability to follow directions is very important for many jobs. These types of questions measure the ability to follow directions by giving a set of rules, which must be followed in answering the questions. *PRINT THE LETTER OF THE CORRECT ANSWER IN THE SPACE AT THE RIGHT.*

RULES

The three types of storage are regular, warehouse, and special. Listed below are the rules for deciding which type of storage to use.

- Regular or warehouse storage should be used for items that do not need special handling.
- Special storage should be used for items that need special handling.
- Warehouse storage should be used for items weighing over 200 pounds.
- Regular storage should be used for items weighing under 200 pounds.
- Special storage should always be used for storing hazardous materials.

Codes:
    1 – Special
    2 – Warehouse
    3 - Regular

1. What type of storage would be used for equipment weighing 350 pounds? 1.____
    A. Special   B. Warehouse   C. Regular

2. What type of storage would be used for a fifty-pound box of dynamite? 2.____
    A. Special   B. Warehouse   C. Regular

3. What type of storage would be used for a five-gallon drum needing refrigeration? 3.____
    A. Special   B. Warehouse   C. Regular

4. What type of storage would be used for machinery weighing 175 pounds? 4.____
    A. Special   B. Warehouse   C. Regular

5. What type of storage would be used for a cement truck used for parts? 5.____
    A. Special   B. Warehouse   C. Regular

KEY (CORRECT ANSWERS)

1. The correct answer is B, Warehouse, because according to the third rule, warehouse storage should be used for items weighing over 200 pounds.

2. The correct answer is A, Special, because the last rule states that special storage should always be used for storing hazardous materials.

3. The correct answer is A, Special, because the item needs the special handling of refrigeration.

4. The correct answer is C, Regular, because the item weighs less than 200 pounds.

5. The correct answer is B, Warehouse, because a cement truck weighs more than 200 pounds.

HOW TO TAKE A TEST

You have studied long, hard and conscientiously.

With your official admission card in hand, and your heart pounding, you have been admitted to the examination room.

You note that there are several hundred other applicants in the examination room waiting to take the same test.

They all appear to be equally well prepared.

You know that nothing but your best effort will suffice. The "moment of truth" is at hand: you now have to demonstrate objectively, in writing, your knowledge of content and your understanding of subject matter.

You are fighting the most important battle of your life—to pass and/or score high on an examination which will determine your career and provide the economic basis for your livelihood.

What extra, special things should you know and should you do in taking the examination?

I. YOU MUST PASS AN EXAMINATION

A. WHAT EVERY CANDIDATE SHOULD KNOW
Examination applicants often ask us for help in preparing for the written test. What can I study in advance? What kinds of questions will be asked? How will the test be given? How will the papers be graded?

B. HOW ARE EXAMS DEVELOPED?
Examinations are carefully written by trained technicians who are specialists in the field known as "psychological measurement," in consultation with recognized authorities in the field of work that the test will cover. These experts recommend the subject matter areas or skills to be tested; only those knowledges or skills important to your success on the job are included. The most reliable books and source materials available are used as references. Together, the experts and technicians judge the difficulty level of the questions.
Test technicians know how to phrase questions so that the problem is clearly stated. Their ethics do not permit "trick" or "catch" questions. Questions may have been tried out on sample groups, or subjected to statistical analysis, to determine their usefulness.
Written tests are often used in combination with performance tests, ratings of training and experience, and oral interviews. All of these measures combine to form the best-known means of finding the right person for the right job.

II. HOW TO PASS THE WRITTEN TEST

A. BASIC STEPS

1) Study the announcement

How, then, can you know what subjects to study? Our best answer is: "Learn as much as possible about the class of positions for which you've applied." The exam will test the knowledge, skills and abilities needed to do the work.

Your most valuable source of information about the position you want is the official exam announcement. This announcement lists the training and experience qualifications. Check these standards and apply only if you come reasonably close to meeting them. Many jurisdictions preview the written test in the exam announcement by including a section called "Knowledge and Abilities Required," "Scope of the Examination," or some similar heading. Here you will find out specifically what fields will be tested.

2) Choose appropriate study materials

If the position for which you are applying is technical or advanced, you will read more advanced, specialized material. If you are already familiar with the basic principles of your field, elementary textbooks would waste your time. Concentrate on advanced textbooks and technical periodicals. Think through the concepts and review difficult problems in your field.

These are all general sources. You can get more ideas on your own initiative, following these leads. For example, training manuals and publications of the government agency which employs workers in your field can be useful, particularly for technical and professional positions. A letter or visit to the government department involved may result in more specific study suggestions, and certainly will provide you with a more definite idea of the exact nature of the position you are seeking.

3) Study this book!

III. KINDS OF TESTS

Tests are used for purposes other than measuring knowledge and ability to perform specified duties. For some positions, it is equally important to test ability to make adjustments to new situations or to profit from training. In others, basic mental abilities not dependent on information are essential. Questions which test these things may not appear as pertinent to the duties of the position as those which test for knowledge and information. Yet they are often highly important parts of a fair examination. For very general questions, it is almost impossible to help you direct your study efforts. What we can do is to point out some of the more common of these general abilities needed in public service positions and describe some typical questions.

1) General information

Broad, general information has been found useful for predicting job success in some kinds of work. This is tested in a variety of ways, from vocabulary lists to questions about current events. Basic background in some field of work, such as sociology or economics, may be sampled in a group of questions. Often these are principles which have become familiar to most persons through exposure rather than through formal training. It is difficult to advise you how to study for these questions; being alert to the world around you is our best suggestion.

2) Verbal ability

An example of an ability needed in many positions is verbal or language ability. Verbal ability is, in brief, the ability to use and understand words. Vocabulary and grammar tests are typical measures of this ability. Reading comprehension or paragraph interpretation questions are common in many kinds of civil service tests. You are given a paragraph of written material and asked to find its central meaning.

IV. KINDS OF QUESTIONS

1. Multiple-choice Questions

Most popular of the short-answer questions is the "multiple choice" or "best answer" question. It can be used, for example, to test for factual knowledge, ability to solve problems or judgment in meeting situations found at work.

A multiple-choice question is normally one of three types:
- It can begin with an incomplete statement followed by several possible endings. You are to find the one ending which best completes the statement, although some of the others may not be entirely wrong.
- It can also be a complete statement in the form of a question which is answered by choosing one of the statements listed.
- It can be in the form of a problem – again you select the best answer.

Here is an example of a multiple-choice question with a discussion which should give you some clues as to the method for choosing the right answer:

When an employee has a complaint about his assignment, the action which will best help him overcome his difficulty is to
    A. discuss his difficulty with his coworkers
    B. take the problem to the head of the organization
    C. take the problem to the person who gave him the assignment
    D. say nothing to anyone about his complaint

In answering this question, you should study each of the choices to find which is best. Consider choice "A" – Certainly an employee may discuss his complaint with fellow employees, but no change or improvement can result, and the complaint remains unresolved. Choice "B" is a poor choice since the head of the organization probably does not know what assignment you have been given, and taking your problem to him is known as "going over the head" of the supervisor. The supervisor, or person who made the assignment, is the person who can clarify it or correct any injustice. Choice "C" is, therefore, correct. To say nothing, as in choice "D," is unwise. Supervisors have and interest in knowing the problems employees are facing, and the employee is seeking a solution to his problem.

2. True/False

3. Matching Questions

Matching an answer from a column of choices within another column.

V. RECORDING YOUR ANSWERS

Computer terminals are used more and more today for many different kinds of exams.

For an examination with very few applicants, you may be told to record your answers in the test booklet itself. Separate answer sheets are much more common. If this separate answer sheet is to be scored by machine – and this is often the case – it is highly important that you mark your answers correctly in order to get credit.

VI. BEFORE THE TEST

YOUR PHYSICAL CONDITION IS IMPORTANT

If you are not well, you can't do your best work on tests. If you are half asleep, you can't do your best either. Here are some tips:

1) Get about the same amount of sleep you usually get. Don't stay up all night before the test, either partying or worrying—DON'T DO IT!
2) If you wear glasses, be sure to wear them when you go to take the test. This goes for hearing aids, too.
3) If you have any physical problems that may keep you from doing your best, be sure to tell the person giving the test. If you are sick or in poor health, you relay cannot do your best on any test. You can always come back and take the test some other time.

Common sense will help you find procedures to follow to get ready for an examination. Too many of us, however, overlook these sensible measures. Indeed, nervousness and fatigue have been found to be the most serious reasons why applicants fail to do their best on civil service tests. Here is a list of reminders:

- Begin your preparation early – Don't wait until the last minute to go scurrying around for books and materials or to find out what the position is all about.
- Prepare continuously – An hour a night for a week is better than an all-night cram session. This has been definitely established. What is more, a night a week for a month will return better dividends than crowding your study into a shorter period of time.
- Locate the place of the exam – You have been sent a notice telling you when and where to report for the examination. If the location is in a different town or otherwise unfamiliar to you, it would be well to inquire the best route and learn something about the building.
- Relax the night before the test – Allow your mind to rest. Do not study at all that night. Plan some mild recreation or diversion; then go to bed early and get a good night's sleep.
- Get up early enough to make a leisurely trip to the place for the test – This way unforeseen events, traffic snarls, unfamiliar buildings, etc. will not upset you.
- Dress comfortably – A written test is not a fashion show. You will be known by number and not by name, so wear something comfortable.
- Leave excess paraphernalia at home – Shopping bags and odd bundles will get in your way. You need bring only the items mentioned in the official notice you received; usually everything you need is provided. Do not bring reference books to the exam. They will only confuse those last minutes and be taken away from you when in the test room.

- Arrive somewhat ahead of time – If because of transportation schedules you must get there very early, bring a newspaper or magazine to take your mind off yourself while waiting.
- Locate the examination room – When you have found the proper room, you will be directed to the seat or part of the room where you will sit. Sometimes you are given a sheet of instructions to read while you are waiting. Do not fill out any forms until you are told to do so; just read them and be prepared.
- Relax and prepare to listen to the instructions
- If you have any physical problem that may keep you from doing your best, be sure to tell the test administrator. If you are sick or in poor health, you really cannot do your best on the exam. You can come back and take the test some other time.

VII. AT THE TEST

The day of the test is here and you have the test booklet in your hand. The temptation to get going is very strong. Caution! There is more to success than knowing the right answers. You must know how to identify your papers and understand variations in the type of short-answer question used in this particular examination. Follow these suggestions for maximum results from your efforts:

1) Cooperate with the monitor

The test administrator has a duty to create a situation in which you can be as much at ease as possible. He will give instructions, tell you when to begin, check to see that you are marking your answer sheet correctly, and so on. He is not there to guard you, although he will see that your competitors do not take unfair advantage. He wants to help you do your best.

2) Listen to all instructions

Don't jump the gun! Wait until you understand all directions. In most civil service tests you get more time than you need to answer the questions. So don't be in a hurry. Read each word of instructions until you clearly understand the meaning. Study the examples, listen to all announcements and follow directions. Ask questions if you do not understand what to do.

3) Identify your papers

Civil service exams are usually identified by number only. You will be assigned a number; you must not put your name on your test papers. Be sure to copy your number correctly. Since more than one exam may be given, copy your exact examination title.

4) Plan your time

Unless you are told that a test is a "speed" or "rate of work" test, speed itself is usually not important. Time enough to answer all the questions will be provided, but this does not mean that you have all day. An overall time limit has been set. Divide the total time (in minutes) by the number of questions to determine the approximate time you have for each question.

5) Do not linger over difficult questions

If you come across a difficult question, mark it with a paper clip (useful to have along) and come back to it when you have been through the booklet. One caution if you do this – be sure to skip a number on your answer sheet as well. Check often to be sure that you have not lost your place and that you are marking in the row numbered the same as the question you are answering.

6) Read the questions

Be sure you know what the question asks! Many capable people are unsuccessful because they failed to read the questions correctly.

7) Answer all questions

Unless you have been instructed that a penalty will be deducted for incorrect answers, it is better to guess than to omit a question.

8) Speed tests

It is often better NOT to guess on speed tests. It has been found that on timed tests people are tempted to spend the last few seconds before time is called in marking answers at random – without even reading them – in the hope of picking up a few extra points. To discourage this practice, the instructions may warn you that your score will be "corrected" for guessing. That is, a penalty will be applied. The incorrect answers will be deducted from the correct ones, or some other penalty formula will be used.

9) Review your answers

If you finish before time is called, go back to the questions you guessed or omitted to give them further thought. Review other answers if you have time.

10) Return your test materials

If you are ready to leave before others have finished or time is called, take ALL your materials to the monitor and leave quietly. Never take any test material with you. The monitor can discover whose papers are not complete, and taking a test booklet may be grounds for disqualification.

VIII. EXAMINATION TECHNIQUES

1) Read the general instructions carefully. These are usually printed on the first page of the exam booklet. As a rule, these instructions refer to the timing of the examination; the fact that you should not start work until the signal and must stop work at a signal, etc. If there are any special instructions, such as a choice of questions to be answered, make sure that you note this instruction carefully.

2) When you are ready to start work on the examination, that is as soon as the signal has been given, read the instructions to each question booklet, underline any key words or phrases, such as least, best, outline, describe and the like. In this way you will tend to answer as requested rather than discover on reviewing your paper that you listed without describing, that you selected the worst choice rather than the best choice, etc.

3) If the examination is of the objective or multiple-choice type – that is, each question will also give a series of possible answers: A, B, C or D, and you are called upon to select the best answer and write the letter next to that answer on your answer paper – it is advisable to start answering each question in turn. There may be anywhere from 50 to 100 such questions in the three or four hours allotted and you can see how much time would be taken if you read through all the questions before beginning to answer any. Furthermore, if you

come across a question or group of questions which you know would be difficult to answer, it would undoubtedly affect your handling of all the other questions.

4) If the examination is of the essay type and contains but a few questions, it is a moot point as to whether you should read all the questions before starting to answer any one. Of course, if you are given a choice – say five out of seven and the like – then it is essential to read all the questions so you can eliminate the two that are most difficult. If, however, you are asked to answer all the questions, there may be danger in trying to answer the easiest one first because you may find that you will spend too much time on it. The best technique is to answer the first question, then proceed to the second, etc.

5) Time your answers. Before the exam begins, write down the time it started, then add the time allowed for the examination and write down the time it must be completed, then divide the time available somewhat as follows:
   - If 3-1/2 hours are allowed, that would be 210 minutes. If you have 80 objective-type questions, that would be an average of 2-1/2 minutes per question. Allow yourself no more than 2 minutes per question, or a total of 160 minutes, which will permit about 50 minutes to review.
   - If for the time allotment of 210 minutes there are 7 essay questions to answer, that would average about 30 minutes a question. Give yourself only 25 minutes per question so that you have about 35 minutes to review.

6) The most important instruction is to read each question and make sure you know what is wanted. The second most important instruction is to time yourself properly so that you answer every question. The third most important instruction is to answer every question. Guess if you have to but include something for each question. Remember that you will receive no credit for a blank and will probably receive some credit if you write something in answer to an essay question. If you guess a letter – say "B" for a multiple-choice question – you may have guessed right. If you leave a blank as an answer to a multiple-choice question, the examiners may respect your feelings but it will not add a point to your score. Some exams may penalize you for wrong answers, so in such cases only, you may not want to guess unless you have some basis for your answer.

7) Suggestions
   a. Objective-type questions
      1. Examine the question booklet for proper sequence of pages and questions
      2. Read all instructions carefully
      3. Skip any question which seems too difficult; return to it after all other questions have been answered
      4. Apportion your time properly; do not spend too much time on any single question or group of questions
      5. Note and underline key words – all, most, fewest, least, best, worst, same, opposite, etc.
      6. Pay particular attention to negatives
      7. Note unusual option, e.g., unduly long, short, complex, different or similar in content to the body of the question
      8. Observe the use of "hedging" words – probably, may, most likely, etc.

9. Make sure that your answer is put next to the same number as the question
10. Do not second-guess unless you have good reason to believe the second answer is definitely more correct
11. Cross out original answer if you decide another answer is more accurate; do not erase until you are ready to hand your paper in
12. Answer all questions; guess unless instructed otherwise
13. Leave time for review

b. Essay questions
   1. Read each question carefully
   2. Determine exactly what is wanted. Underline key words or phrases.
   3. Decide on outline or paragraph answer
   4. Include many different points and elements unless asked to develop any one or two points or elements
   5. Show impartiality by giving pros and cons unless directed to select one side only
   6. Make and write down any assumptions you find necessary to answer the questions
   7. Watch your English, grammar, punctuation and choice of words
   8. Time your answers; don't crowd material

8) Answering the essay question

Most essay questions can be answered by framing the specific response around several key words or ideas. Here are a few such key words or ideas:

M's: manpower, materials, methods, money, management
P's: purpose, program, policy, plan, procedure, practice, problems, pitfalls, personnel, public relations

a. Six basic steps in handling problems:
   1. Preliminary plan and background development
   2. Collect information, data and facts
   3. Analyze and interpret information, data and facts
   4. Analyze and develop solutions as well as make recommendations
   5. Prepare report and sell recommendations
   6. Install recommendations and follow up effectiveness

b. Pitfalls to avoid
1. Taking things for granted – A statement of the situation does not necessarily imply that each of the elements is necessarily true; for example, a complaint may be invalid and biased so that all that can be taken for granted is that a complaint has been registered
2. Considering only one side of a situation – Wherever possible, indicate several alternatives and then point out the reasons you selected the best one
3. Failing to indicate follow up – Whenever your answer indicates action on your part, make certain that you will take proper follow-up action to see how successful your recommendations, procedures or actions turn out to be
4. Taking too long in answering any single question – Remember to time your answers properly

EXAMINATION SECTION

WRITTEN ENGLISH EXPRESSION
EXAMINATION SECTION
TEST 1

DIRECTIONS: In each of the sentences below, four portions are underlined and lettered. Read each sentence and decide whether any of the UNDERLINED parts contains an error in spelling, punctuation, or capitalization, or employs grammatical usage which would be inappropriate for carefully written English. If so, note the letter printed under the unacceptable form and indicate this choice in the space at the right. If all four of the underlined portions are acceptable as they stand, select the answer E. (No sentence contains more than ONE unacceptable form.)

1. The revised <u>procedure</u> was <u>quite</u> different <u>than</u> the one which <u>was</u> employed up to that time. <u>No error</u>
         A   B   C   D   E

1.____

2. <u>Blinded</u> by the storm that <u>surrounded</u> him, his plane <u>kept going</u> in <u>circles</u>. <u>No error</u>

2.____

3. They <u>should</u> give the book to <u>whoever</u> <u>they</u> think deserves <u>it</u>. <u>No error</u>
         A   B C   D E

3.____

4. The <u>government</u> will not consent to your <u>firm</u> <u>sending</u> that package as <u>second class</u> matter. <u>No error</u>

4.____

5. She <u>would have</u> avoided all the trouble <u>that</u> followed if she <u>would have</u> waited ten minutes <u>longer</u>. <u>No error</u>

5.____

6. <u>His</u> poetry, <u>when</u> it was carefully examined, showed <u>characteristics</u> not unlike Wordsworth. <u>No error</u>

6.____

7. <u>In my opinion</u>, based upon long years of research, <u>I think</u> the plan offered by my opponent is <u>unsound</u>, because it is not <u>founded</u> on true facts. <u>No error</u>

7.____

8. The soldiers of <u>Washington's</u> army at Valley Forge <u>were</u> men ragged in
       A   B
   <u>appearance</u> but <u>who were</u> noble in character. <u>No error</u>
       C   D   E

9. Rabbits <u>have a distrust</u> of man <u>due to</u> the fact <u>that</u> they are <u>so often</u> shot.
              A   B   C   D
   <u>No error</u>
   E

10. <u>This</u> is the man <u>who</u> I believe <u>is</u> best <u>qualified</u> for the position. <u>No error</u>
     A   B   C   D   E

11. Her voice was <u>not only</u> <u>good</u>, but <u>she</u> also very clearly <u>enunciated</u>.
                    A   B   C   D
    <u>No error</u>
    E

12. <u>Today he</u> is wearing a <u>different</u> suit <u>than</u> the <u>one</u> he wore yesterday. <u>No error</u>
     A   B   C   D   E

13. Our work <u>is</u> to improve the club; if anybody <u>must</u> resign, let it <u>not</u> be you or <u>I</u>.
              A   B   C   D
    <u>No error</u>
    E

14. There was so much talking <u>in back of</u> me <u>as</u> I <u>could</u> not <u>enjoy</u> the music.
                                 A   B   C   D
    <u>No error</u>
    E

15. <u>Being that</u> he is that <u>kind of</u> <u>boy</u>, he cannot be blamed <u>for</u> the mistake.
     A   B   C   D
    <u>No error</u>
    E

16. <u>The king, having read</u> the speech, <u>he</u> and the <u>queen</u> <u>departed</u>. <u>No error</u>
     A   B   C   D   E

17. I <u>am</u> <u>so tired</u> I <u>can't</u> <u>scarcely</u> stand. <u>No error</u>
       A   B   C   D   E

18. We are <u>mailing bills</u> to our customers <u>in Canada</u>, and, <u>being</u> eager to
                A   B   C
    clear our books before the new season opens, it is <u>to be hoped</u> they will
                                                            D
    send their remittances promptly. <u>No error</u>
                                            E

19. I reluctantly acquiesced to the proposal. No error
    A   B   C   D   E

20. It had lain out in the rain all night. No error
    A B   C   D   E

21. If he would have gone there, he would have seen a marvelous sight.
              A   B   C   D
    No error
    E

22. The climate of Asia Minor is somewhat like Utah. No error
                 A   B   C   D   E

23. If everybody did unto others as they would wish others to do unto them, this
        A   B   C   D
    world would be a paradise. No error
                                E

24. This was the jockey whom I saw was most likely to win the race. No error
    A   B   C   D   E

25. The only food the general demanded was potatoes. No error
        A   B   C   D   E

KEY (CORRECT ANSWERS)

1.	C	11.	C
2.	A	12.	C
3.	B	13.	D
4.	B	14.	B
5.	C	15.	A
6.	D	16.	A
7.	B	17.	C
8.	D	18.	C
9.	B	19.	E
10.	E	20.	E

21.	A
22.	D
23.	D
24.	B
25.	E

TEST 2

DIRECTIONS: In each of the sentences below, four portions are underlined and lettered. Read each sentence and decide whether any of the UNDERLINED parts contains an error in spelling, punctuation, or capitalization, or employs grammatical usage which would be inappropriate for carefully written English. If so, note the letter printed under the unacceptable form and indicate this choice in the space at the right. If all four of the underlined portions are acceptable as they stand, select the answer E. (No sentence contains more than ONE unacceptable form.)

1. A party <u>like</u> <u>that</u> <u>only</u> <u>comes</u> once a year. <u>No error</u>   1.____
           A   B   C   D   E

2. <u>Our's</u> <u>is</u> <u>a</u> <u>swift moving</u> age. <u>No error</u>   2.____
     A   B C   D   E

3. The <u>healthy</u> climate soon <u>restored</u> him <u>to</u> his <u>accustomed</u> vigor. <u>No error</u>   3.____
         A   B   C   D   E

4. <u>They</u> needed six typists and hoped that <u>only</u> that <u>many</u> <u>would</u> apply for the   4.____
    A   B   C   D
   position. <u>No error</u>
                 E

5. He <u>interviewed</u> people <u>whom</u> he thought had <u>something</u> <u>to impart</u>. <u>No error</u>   5.____
           A   B   C   D   E

6. <u>Neither</u> of his three sisters <u>is</u> older <u>than</u> <u>he</u>. <u>No error</u>   6.____
     A   B   C D   E

7. <u>Since</u> he is <u>that</u> <u>kind</u> of <u>a</u> boy, he cannot be expected to cooperate with us.   7.____
     A   B   C   D
   <u>No error</u>
     E

8. <u>When passing</u> <u>through</u> the tunnel, the air pressure <u>affected</u> <u>our</u> years. <u>No error</u>   8.____
       A   B   C   D   E

9. <u>The story having</u> a sad ending, <u>it</u> never <u>achieved</u> popularity <u>among</u> the   9.____
         A   B   C   D
   students. <u>No error</u>
               E

10. <u>Since</u> we are both hungry, <u>shall</u> we go <u>somewhere</u> for lunch? <u>No error</u>   10.____
       A   B   C   D E

11. Will you please bring this book down to the library and give it to my friend, who is waiting for it? No error
    A   B   C   D
                                                                                                    E

12. You may have the book; I am finished with it. No error
         A   B   C   D   E

13. I don't know if I should mention it to her or not. No error
       A   B   C   D   E

14. Philosophy is not a subject which has to do with philosophers and mathematics only. No error
                      A   B   C   D   E

15. The thoughts of the scholar in his library are little different than the old woman who first said, "It's no use crying over spilt milk." No error
                                    A   B
                                          C   D   E

16. A complete system of philosophical ideas are implied in many simple utterances. No error
                    A   B   C   D   E

17. Even if one has never put them into words, his ideas compose a kind of a philosophy. No error
           A   B   C   D   E

18. Perhaps it is well enough that most people do not attempt this formulation. No error
              A   B   C   D   E

19. Leading their ordered lives, this confused body of ideas and feelings is sufficient. No error
        A   B   C   D   E

20. Why should we insist upon them formulating it? No error
          A   B   C   D   E

21. Since it includes something of the wisdom of the ages, it is adequate for the purposes of ordinary life. No error
      A   B   C
          D   E

22. Therefore, I have sought to make a pattern of mine, and so there were, early   22.____
        A   B   C
    moments of my trying to find out what were the elements with which I had to
                 D
    deal. No error
          E

23. I wanted to get what knowledge I could about the general structure of the   23.____
        A   B   C   D
    universe. No error
              E

24. I wanted to know if life per se had any meaning or whether I must strive to give   24.____
                A B   C   D
    it one. No error
            E

25. So, in a desultory way, I began to read. No error   25.____
    A   B   C   D   E

KEY (CORRECT ANSWERS)

1.	C		11.	B
2.	A		12.	C
3.	A		13.	B
4.	C		14.	D
5.	B		15.	B
6.	A		16.	B
7.	D		17.	A
8.	A		18.	C
9.	A		19.	A
10.	E		20.	D

21. E
22. C
23. C
24. B
25. E

WRITTEN ENGLISH EXPRESSION
EXAMINATION SECTION
TEST 1

DIRECTIONS: In each of the sentences below, four portions are underlined and lettered. Read each sentence and decide whether any of the underlined parts contains an error in spelling, punctuation, or capitalization, or employs grammatical usage which would be inappropriate for carefully written English. If so, note the letter printed under the unacceptable form and print it in the space at the right. If all four of the underlined portions are acceptable as they stand, print the letter E. No sentences contains more than one unacceptable form.

1. A low ceiling <u>is</u> <u>when</u> the atmospheric conditions <u>make</u> <u>flying</u> inadvisable.   1.____
                A   B   C   D

2. <u>They</u> couldn't <u>tell</u> <u>who</u> the card was <u>from</u>.   2.____
   A   B C   D

3. No one <u>but</u> you and <u>I</u> <u>are</u> to <u>help</u> them.   3.____
        A   B C   D

4. To <u>him</u> <u>fall</u> the <u>duties</u> of <u>foster parent</u>.   4.____
     A. B.   C   D

5. If the word <u>should</u> somehow find peace <u>within itself</u>, so that all <u>her</u> people   5.____
              A   B   C
<u>would</u> stop fighting everlastingly…that would be the day!
D

6. <u>Everyone</u> of the <u>teachers</u> prepared <u>his</u> lesson in a <u>consummate</u> manner.   6.____
    A   B   C   D

7. <u>Didn't</u> <u>they</u> <u>used</u> to <u>pay</u> promptly?   7.____
   A   B   C   D

8. The services <u>rendered</u> by these people and <u>their</u> share <u>in making</u> the work a   8.____
                      A   B   C
success <u>is</u> to be commended.
D

9. <u>They</u> <u>couldn't</u> tell <u>whom</u> the cable was <u>recieved</u> from…   9.____
   A   B   C   D

10. We like <u>these</u> <u>better</u> than <u>those</u> <u>kind</u>.   10.____
          A   B   C D

2 (#1)

11. It is a test of you more than I.
    A   B   C   D   11.____

12. The person in charge being him there can be no change in policy.
         A   B   C   D   12.____

13. A large amount of information and news are to be found there.
      A   B   C   D   13.____

14. I should have liked to have seen it again.
        A   B   C D   14.____

15. The desire to travel made him restless.
                A   B   C   D   15.____

16. Should that effect their decision?
      A   B   C   D   16.____

17. Do as we do for the celebration of the childrens' event.
    A B   C   D   17.____

18. Do either of you care to join us?
    A   B   C   D   18.____

19. A child's food requirements differ from the adult.
       A   B   C   D   19.____

20. A large family, including two uncles and four grandparents live at the hotel.
             A   B   C D   20.____

21. If they would have done that, they might have succeeded.
              A   B   C   D   21.____

22. Neither the hot days or the humid nights annoy our Southern visitor.
       A   B   C   D   22.____

23. Some people do not gain favor because they are kind of tactless.
     A   B   C   D   23.____

24. No sooner had the turning point come than a new embarassing issue arose.
        A   B   C   D   24.____

25. An usher seldom rises above a theatre manager.
              A   B   C   D   25.____

KEY (CORRECT ANSWERS)

1.	B		11.	D
2.	C		12.	C
3.	B		13.	C
4.	E		14.	B
5.	C		15.	E
6.	D		16.	B
7.	C		17.	D
8.	D		18.	A
9.	D		19.	D
10.	C		20.	C

21. A
22. B
23. D
24. D
25. C

TEST 2

DIRECTIONS: In each of the sentences below, four portions are underlined and lettered. Read each sentence and decide whether any of the underlined parts contains an error in spelling, punctuation, or capitalization, or employs grammatical usage which would be inappropriate for carefully written English. If so, note the letter printed under the unacceptable form and print it in the space at the right. If all four of the underlined portions are acceptable as they stand, print the letter E. No sentences contains more than one unacceptable form.

1. The <u>epic</u>, "Gone With the Wind<u>,"</u> deals with events that <u>ocurred</u> during the Civil War <u>era</u>.
    A   B   C
                  D

   1.____

2. <u>Shall</u> you <u>be at home,</u> <u>let us say</u>, on Sunday at two o'clock?
    A   B   C   D

   2.____

3. We <u>see</u> Mr. <u>Lewis'</u> <u>take</u> his car <u>out of the garage</u> daily.
     A   B   C   D

   3.____

4. We <u>have</u> <u>no</u> place <u>to keep</u> our rubbers, <u>only</u> in the hall closet.
     A B   C   D

   4.____

5. <u>Isn't it true</u> <u>what</u> <u>you</u> <u>told</u> me about the best way to prepare for an examination?
   A   B C D

   5.____

6. "<u>Who</u> <u>shall</u> I say called," the butler <u>asked</u> <u>?</u>
    A   B   C D

   6.____

7. The museum <u>is</u> often visited by students who <u>are</u> fond of <u>Primitive</u> paintings, and by <u>patent</u> attorneys.
             A   B   C

   7.____

8. I <u>rose to nominate</u> the <u>superintendant,</u> the man <u>who</u> most of us felt was the best.
   A   B   C   D

   8.____

9. The child <u>was</u> sent to the store to <u>purchase</u> a bottle of milk and <u>brought</u> home fresh rolls, <u>too</u>.
           A   B   C
                        D

   9.____

10. The garden tool <u>was sent</u> <u>to be sharpened</u> and a new handle <u>to be</u> <u>put on</u>.
                     A   B   C D

   10.____

11. At the end of her vacation, Joan came home with little money, nevertheless, 11._____
                                                             A   B   C
    it was a joyous occasion.
                    D

12. We people have opportunities to show the rest of the world how real 12._____
          A   B
    democracy functions and leads to the perfectability of man.
                                    C   D

13. The guide paddled along and then fell into a reverie where he related the 13._____
                                          A   B   C   D
    history of the region.

14. We should have investigated the cause of the noise in the Hotel by bringing 14._____
            A   B   C   D
    the car to a halt.

15. The first few strokes of the brush were enough to convince me that Tom 15._____
                                          A   B
    could paint much better than me.
                C   D

16. We inquired whether we could see the owner of the store, after we waited 16._____
                  A   B   C
    for one hour.
        D

17. The irratation of the high-strung parent was aggravated by the slightest 17._____
            A   B   C
    noise that the baby made.
                         D

18. There is a large demand for men interested in the field of Information Retrieval. 18._____
          A B   C   D

19. Snow after the rains delay the coming crops. 19._____
       A   B   C   D

20. They intend to partially do away with ceremonies. 20._____
      A   B   C   D

21. If that be done and turns out badly we shall see horror. 21._____
      A   B   C   D

22. The new plant is to be electrically lighted; increasing brightness by 50%. 22._____
             A   B   C   D

3 (#2)

23. The <u>reason</u> the speaker was offended <u>was</u> <u>that</u> the audience <u>was</u> inattentive. 23._____
     A   B C   D

24. There <u>appear</u> <u>to be</u> conditions <u>that</u> govern the behavioral <u>Sciences.</u> 24._____
          A   B   C   D

25. <u>Either</u> of the men <u>are</u> influential <u>enough</u> <u>to control</u> the situation. 25._____
     A   B   C   D

KEY (CORRECT ANSWERS)

1.	C	11.	A
2.	E	12.	D
3.	B	13.	C
4.	D	14.	C
5.	B	15.	D
6.	D	16.	C
7.	C	17.	A
8.	C	18.	D
9.	C	19.	C
10.	C	20.	E

21. C
22. C
23. E
24. D
25. B

TEST 3

DIRECTIONS: In each of the sentences below, four portions are underlined and lettered. Read each sentence and decide whether any of the underlined parts contains an error in spelling, punctuation, or capitalization, or employs grammatical usage which would be inappropriate for carefully written English. If so, note the letter printed under the unacceptable form and print it in the space at the right. If all four of the underlined portions are acceptable as they stand, print the letter E. No sentences contains more than one unacceptable form.

1. <u>Who</u> <u>did</u> you predict <u>would win</u> the election <u>this</u> year?   1.____
    A   B   C   D

2. <u>It</u> takes a <u>lot</u> <u>more</u> effort <u>to sell</u> houses this year than last year.   2.____
    A   B C   D

3. <u>Having pranced</u> into the arena <u>with little grace and unsteady hoof</u>   3.____
          A   B
   <u>for the jumps ahead,</u> <u>the driver reined his horse</u>.
           C   D

4. Once the dog wagged <u>it's</u> tail, <u>you</u> knew <u>it</u> <u>was</u> a friendly animal.   4.____
                                  A   B   C D

5. The record of the winning team was <u>among</u> the <u>most</u> <u>noteworthy</u>   5.____
                                           A   B   C
   <u>of the season</u>.
      D

6. <u>When</u> <u>asked</u> to choose corn, cabbage, <u>or</u> potatoes, the diner selected the   6.____
     A   B   C
   <u>latter.</u>
    D

7. The maid <u>wasn't</u> <u>so</u> small <u>that</u> she <u>couldn't</u> reach the top window for cleaning.   7.____
                A   B   C   D

8. Many people <u>feel</u> that powdered coffee <u>produces</u> a <u>really</u> <u>abhorent</u> flavor.   8.____
                 A   B   C   D

9. <u>Would you mind</u> <u>me</u> <u>trying</u> that coat on for <u>size?</u>   9.____
        A   B C   D

10. This chair <u>looks</u> <u>much</u> <u>different</u> <u>than</u> the chair we selected in the store.   10.____
               A   B   C   D

11. After <u>trying</u> unsuccessfully <u>to land</u> a <u>job</u> in the city, Will <u>settled</u> in the   11.____
          A   B   C   D
    country on a farm.

12. On the last attempt, the pole-vaulter <u>came</u> <u>nearly</u> <u>to getting</u> <u>hurt.</u>   12._____
                                                                                A   B   C   D

13. The <u>observance</u> of <u>armistice day</u> <u>throughout the world</u> offers an opportunity   13._____
                A   B   C

    <u>to reflect</u> on the horrors of war.
     D

14. <u>Outside of</u> the mistakes in spelling, the child's letter <u>was</u> a <u>very</u> good <u>one.</u>   14._____
        A   B   C   D

15. <u>Scisors</u> <u>are</u> always dangerous <u>for</u> a child to <u>handle.</u>   15._____
      A   B   C   D

16. I assure <u>you</u> <u>that</u> I <u>will not yield</u> to pressure <u>to sell</u> my interest.   16._____
               A   B   C   D

17. Ask <u>him</u> if he <u>recalls</u> the incident which <u>took place</u> at our first meeting.   17._____
         A B   C   D

18. The manager <u>felt like as not to order</u> his <u>usher-captain</u> <u>to surrender</u> his   18._____
                           A   B   C   D

    uniform.

19. The mother of the bride <u>climaxed</u> the <u>occasion</u> <u>by exclaiming,</u> "I want my   19._____
                                    A   B   C

    children <u>should</u> be happy forever."
            D

20. We <u>read</u> <u>in the papers</u> <u>where</u> the prospects for peace <u>are</u> improving.   20._____
        A   B   C   D

21. "<u>Can</u> I <u>share</u> the <u>cab</u> with you?" <u>was</u> frequently heard during the period of   21._____
      A   B   C   D

    gas rationing.

22. <u>Had</u> the police <u>suspected</u> the ruse, they <u>would have taken</u> <u>relevant</u>   22._____
     A   B   C   D

    precautions.

23. The teacher admonished the <u>other</u> students <u>neither</u> to speak to John, <u>nor</u>   23._____
                                         A   B   C

    <u>should they</u> annoy him.
        D

24. Fortunately, <u>we had been told</u> <u>that</u> there was <u>but</u> one <u>availible</u> service   24._____
                               A   B   C   D

    station in that area.

25. We haven't hardly enough time to make it. 25._____
     A   B   C   D

KEY (CORRECT ANSWERS)

1.	E		11.	B
2.	B		12.	B
3.	D		13.	B
4.	A		14.	A
5.	E		15.	A
6.	D		16.	E
7.	B		17.	B
8.	D		18.	B
9.	B		19.	D
10.	A		20.	C

21. A
22. D
23. D
24. D
25. A

TEST 4

DIRECTIONS: In each of the sentences below, four portions are underlined and lettered. Read each sentence and decide whether any of the underlined parts contains an error in spelling, punctuation, or capitalization, or employs grammatical usage which would be inappropriate for carefully written English. If so, note the letter printed under the unacceptable form and print it in the space at the right. If all four of the underlined portions are acceptable as they stand, print the letter E. No sentences contains more than one unacceptable form.

1. He <u>either</u> <u>will fail</u> in his attempt <u>or</u> will seek other <u>Government</u> employment.
     A   B   C   D

1._____

2. <u>After</u> each side <u>gave</u> <u>their</u> version, the case <u>was</u> closed.
   A   B C   D

2._____

3. <u>Every</u> <u>one</u> of the cars <u>were</u> <u>tagged</u> by the police.
   A   B   C   D

3._____

4. They <u>can't</u> <u>seem</u> <u>to see</u> <u>it</u> when I explain the theory.
      A   B   C D

4._____

5. <u>It</u> is difficult <u>to find</u> the genuine signature <u>between</u> all <u>those</u> submitted.
  A   B   C   D

5._____

6. She can't understand why <u>they don't remember</u> <u>who</u> to give the letter <u>to</u>.
                                 A   B   C   D

6._____

7. <u>Every</u> <u>man and woman</u> in America <u>is</u> interested in <u>his</u> tax bill.
   A   B   C   D

7._____

8. A guard <u>was called</u> <u>to prevent</u> <u>them</u> <u>carrying away</u> souvenirs.
          A   B   C   D

8._____

9. <u>Neither</u> you <u>nor</u> <u>I</u> <u>am</u> to blame for the sudden slump in business.
   A   B C D

9._____

10. To <u>you</u> and <u>him</u> <u>belong</u> the <u>credit.</u>
     A   B   C   D

10._____

11. The auctioneer had <u>less</u> items to <u>sell</u> this year <u>than</u> last <u>year.</u>
                      A   B   C   D

11._____

12. <u>Theirs</u> <u>instead of</u> <u>his</u> instructions <u>will be followed</u>.
    A   B   C   D

12._____

13. <u>It</u> is the <u>same</u> at his local <u>broker's</u> Frank <u>Smith</u>.
   A   B   C   D

13._____

2 (#4)

14. The teacher <u>politely</u> <u>requested</u> <u>each</u> pupil to <u>step in</u> the room. 14.____
              A   B   C   D

15. <u>Too</u> many parents <u>leave</u> <u>their</u> children do as <u>they</u> please. 15.____
    A   B   C   D

16. <u>He</u> arrived <u>safe,</u> his papers <u>untouched,</u> his composure <u>unrufled.</u> 16.____
    A   B   C   D

17. I <u>do not</u> have <u>any</u> faith in <u>John</u> <u>running</u> for office. 17.____
      A   B   C   D

18. The musicians began to play <u>tunefully</u> ; <u>keeping</u> the proper tempo <u>indicated</u> 18.____
                                   A   B   C   D
for the selection.

19. <u>Mary's</u> maid of honor bought the <u>kind of</u> <u>an</u> <u>outfit</u> suitable for an afternoon 19.____
    A   B   C D
wedding.

20. After the debate, <u>every one</u> of the <u>Speakers</u> realized that, <u>given</u> another 20.____
                       A   B   C
chance, he <u>could have done</u> better.
                D

21. The reason <u>given</u> by the physician for the patient's trouble <u>was</u> <u>because</u> of 21.____
            A   B   C
his poor eating <u>habits</u>.
                  D

22. The fog was so <u>thick</u> that the driver <u>couldn't</u> <u>hardly</u> see more than ten feet 22.____
                   A   B   C
<u>ahead.</u>
D

23. I suggest that you <u>present</u> the medal to <u>who</u> you <u>deem</u> <u>best</u>. 23.____
                      A   B   C   D

24. A decision made by a man <u>without much deliberation</u> is sometimes <u>no</u> 24.____
                                 A   B
different <u>than</u> a <u>slow one</u>.
        C   D

25. <u>By the time</u> Jones <u>graduates from</u> <u>Dental School,</u> he <u>will be</u> twenty-six years 25.____
    A   B   C   D
of age.

KEY (CORRECT ANSWERS)

1.	D	11.	A
2.	C	12.	A
3.	C	13.	D
4.	C	14.	D
5.	C	15.	B
6.	C	16.	D
7.	E	17.	C
8.	C	18.	B
9.	E	19.	C
10.	C	20.	B

21.	C
22.	B
23.	B
24.	D
25.	C

TEST 5

Questions 1-18.

DIRECTIONS: Each of the sentences numbered 1 through 18 may be classified most appropriately under one of the following three categories:
   A. faulty because of incorrect grammar
   B. faulty because of incorrect punctuation
   C. correct

Examine each sentence carefully. Then, in the space at the right, print the letter preceding the option which is BEST of those suggested above. All incorrect sentences contain but one type of error. Consider a sentence correct if it contains none of the types of errors mentioned, even though there may be other correct ways of expressing the same thought.

1. He sent the notice to the clerk who you hired yesterday. 1._____

2. It must be admitted, however that you were not informed of this change. 2._____

3. Only the employees who have served in this grade for at least two years are eligible for promotion. 3._____

4. The work was divided equally between she and Mary. 4._____

5. He thought that you were not available at that time. 5._____

6. When the messenger returns; please give him this package. 6._____

7. The new secretary prepared, typed, addressed, and delivered, the notices. 7._____

8. Walking into the room, his desk can be seen at the rear. 8._____

9. Although John has worked here longer than she, he produces a smaller amount of work. 9._____

10. She said she could of typed this report yesterday. 10._____

11. Neither one of these procedures are adequate for the efficient performance of this task. 11._____

12. The typewriter is the tool of the typist; the cash register, the tool of the cashier. 12._____

13. "The assignment must be completed as soon as possible" said the supervisor. 13._____

14. As you know, office handbooks are issued to all new employees. 14._____

15. Writing a speech is sometimes easier than to deliver it before an audience. 15._____

16. Mr. Brown our accountant, will audit the accounts next week. 16._____

17. Give the assignment to whomever is able to do it most efficiently. 17._____

18. The supervisor expected either your or I to file these reports. 18._____

Questions 19-28.

DIRECTIONS: Each of the following sentences may be classified most appropriately under one of the following four categories:
- A. faulty because of incorrect grammar
- B. faulty because of incorrect punctuation
- C. faulty because of incorrect spelling
- D. correct

Examine each sentence carefully. Then, in the space at the right, print the letter preceding the option which is BEST of those suggested above. All incorrect sentences contain but one type of error. Consider a sentence correct if it contains none of the types of errors mentioned, even though there may be other correct ways of expressing the same thought.

19. The fire apparently started in the storeroom, which is usually locked. 19._____

20. On approaching the victim two bruises were noticed by the officer. 20._____

21. The officer, who was there examined the report with great care. 21._____

22. Each employee in the office had a separate desk. 22._____

23. All employees including members of the clerical staff, were invited to the lecture. 23._____

24. The suggested procedure is similar to the one now in use. 24._____

25. No one was more pleased with the new procedure than the chauffeur. 25._____

26. He tried to pursuade her to change the procedure. 26._____

27. The total of the expenses charged to petty cash were high. 27._____

28. An understanding between him and I was finally reached. 28._____

KEY (CORRECT ANSWERS)

1.	A	11.	A	21.	B
2.	B	12.	C	22.	C
3.	C	13.	B	23.	B
4.	A	14.	C	24.	D
5.	C	15.	A	25.	D
6.	B	16.	B	26.	C
7.	B	17.	A	27.	A
8.	A	18.	A	28.	A
9.	C	19.	D		
10.	A	20.	A		

WRITTEN ENGLISH EXPRESSION
EXAMINATION SECTION
TEST 1

DIRECTIONS: The following questions are designed to test your knowledge of grammar, sentence structure, correct usage, and punctuation. In each group, there is one sentence that contains an error. Select the letter of the INCORRECT sentence. *PRINT THE LETTER OF THE CORRECT ANSWER IN THE SPACE AT THE RIGHT.*

1. A. All things considered, he did unusually well.
    B. The poor boy takes everything too seriously.
    C. Our club sent two delegates, Ruth and I, to Oswego.
    D. I like him better than her.
    E. His eccentricities continually made good newspaper copy.

    1.____

2. A. If we except Benton, no one in the club foresaw the changes.
    B. The two-year-old rosebushes are loaded with buds—and beetles!
    C. Though the pitcher had been broken by the cat, Teena was furious.
    D. Virginia got the cake recipe off of her grandmother.
    E. Neither one of the twins was able to get a summer vacation.

    2.____

3. A. "What do you wish?" he asked, "may I help you?"
    B. Whose gloves are these?
    C. Has he drink all the orange juice?
    D. It was he who spoke to the manager of the store.
    E. Mary prefers this kind of evening dress.

    3.____

4. A. Charles himself said it before the assembled peers of the realm.
    B. The wind stirred the rose petals laying on the floor.
    C. The storm beat hard on the frozen windowpanes.
    D. Worn out by the days of exposure and storm, the sailor clung pitifully to the puny raft.
    E. The day afterward he thought more kindly of the matter.

    4.____

5. A. Between you and me, I think Henry is wrong.
    B. This is the more interesting of the two books.
    C. This is the most carefully written letter of all.
    D. During the opening course I read not only four plays but also three historical novels.
    E. This assortment of candies, nuts, and fruits are excellent.

    5.____

6. A. According to your report card, you are not so clever as he.
    B. If he had kept his eyes open, he would not have fallen into that trap.
    C. We were certain that the horse had broken it's leg.
    D. The troop of scouts and the leader are headed for the North Woods.
    E. I knew it to be him by the knock at the door.

    6.____

7. A. Being one of the earliest spring flowers, we welcome the crocus.
   B. The cold running water became colder as time sped on.
   C. Those boys need not have stood in line for lunch.
   D. Can you, my friend, donate ten dollars to the cause?
   E. Because it's a borrowed umbrella, return it in the morning.

8. A. If Walter would have planted earlier in the spring, the rosebushes would have survived.
   B. The flowers smell overpoweringly sweet.
   C. There are three *e*'s in dependent.
   D. May I be excused at the end of the test?
   E. Carl has three brothers-in-law.

9. A. We have bought neither the lumber nor the tools for the job.
   B. Jefferson was re-elected despite certain powerful opposition.
   C. The Misses Jackson were invited to the dance.
   D. The letter is neither theirs nor yours.
   E. The retail price for those items are far beyond the wholesale quotations.

10. A. To find peace of mind is to gain treasure beyond price.
    B. Fred is cheerful, carefree; his brother is morose.
    C. Whoever fails to understand the strategic importance of the Arctic fails to understand modern geography.
    D. They came promptly at 8 o'clock on August 7, 2020, without prior notification.
    E. Every one tried their best to guess the answer, but no one succeeded.

11. A. Is this hers or theirs?
    B. Having been recognized, Frank took the floor.
    C. Alex invited Sue; Paul, Marion; and Dan, Helen.
    D. If I were able to do the task, you can be sure that I'd do it.
    E. Stamp collecting, or philately as it is otherwise called is truly an international hobby.

12. A. He has proved himself to be reliable.
    B. The fisherman had arisen before the sun.
    C. By the time the truck arrived, I had put out the blaze.
    D. The doctor with his colleagues were engaged in consultation.
    E. I chose to try out a new method, but in spite of my efforts it failed.

13. A. He has drunk too much iced tea.
    B. I appreciated him doing that job for me.
    C. The royal family fled, but they were retaken.
    D. The secretary and the treasurer were both present on Friday,
    E. Iago protested his honesty, yet he continued to plot against Desdemona.

14. A. The family were all together at Easter.
    B. It is altogether too fine a day for us to stay indoors.
    C. However much you dislike him, you should treat him fairly.
    D. The judges were already there when the contestants arrived.
    E. The boy's mother reported that he was alright again after the accident.

15. A. Ham and eggs is a substantial breakfast.
    B. By the end of the week the pond had frozen.
    C. I should appreciate any assistance you could offer me.
    D. Being that tomorrow is Sunday, we expect to close early.
    E. If he were to win the medal, I for one would be disturbed.

16. A. Give the letter to whoever comes for it.
    B. He feels bad, but his sister is the one who looks sicker.
    C. He had an unbelievable large capacity for hard physical work.
    D. Earth has nothing more beautiful to offer than the autumn colors of this section of the country.
    E. Happily we all have hopes that the future will soon bring forth fruits of a lasting peace.

17. A. This kind of apples is my favorite.
    B. Either of the players is capable of performing ably.
    C. Though trying my best to be calm, the choice was not an easy one for me.
    D. The nearest star is not several light years away; it is only 93,000,000 miles away.
    E. There were two things I still wished to do—to see the Lincoln Memorial and to climb up the Washington Monument.

18. A. It is I who is to blame.
    B. That dress looks very good on Jane.
    C. People often take my brother to be me.
    D. I could but think she had deceived me.
    E. He himself told us that the story was true,

19. A. They all went but Mabel and me.
    B. Has he ever swum across the river?
    C. We have a dozen other suggestions besides these.
    D. The Jones's are going to visit their friends in Chicago.
    E. The ideal that Arthur and his knights were in quest of was a better world order.

20. A. Would I were able to be there with you!
    B. Whomever he desires to see should be admitted.
    C. It is not for such as we to follow fashion blindly.
    D. His causing the confusion seemed to affect him not at all.
    E. Please notify all those whom you think should have this information.

21. A. She was not only competent but also friendly in nature.
    B. Not only must we visualize the play we are reading; we must actually hear it.
    C. The firm was not only acquiring a bad reputation but also indulging in illegal practices.
    D. The bank was not only uncooperative but also was indifferent to new business offered them.
    E. I know that a conscious effort was made not only to guard the material but also to keep it from being used.

21.____

22. A. How old shall you be on your next birthday?
    B. I am sure that he has been here and did what was expected of him.
    C. Near to the bank of the river, stood, secluded and still, the house of the hermit.
    D. Because of its efficacy in treating many ailments, penicillin has become an important addition to the druggist's stock.
    E. ROBINSON CRUSOE, which is a fairy tale to the child, is a work of social philosophy to the mature thinker.

22.____

23. A. We had no sooner started than it rained.
    B. The fact that the prisoner is a minor will be taken into consideration.
    C. Many parents think more of their older children than of their younger ones.
    D. The boy laid a book, a knife and a fishing line on the table.
    E. John is the tallest of any boy in his class.

23.____

24. A. Although we have been friend for many years, I must admit that May is most inconsiderate.
    B. He is not able to run, not even to walk.
    C. You will bear this pain as you have so many greater ones.
    D. The harder the work, the more studious she became.
    E. Too many "and's" in a sentence produce an immature style.

24.____

25. A. It would be preferable to have you submit questions after, not before, the lecture.
    B. Plan your work; then work your plan.
    C. At last John met his brother, who had been waiting two hours for him.
    D. Should one penalize ones self for not trying?
    E. There are other considerations besides this one.

25.____

KEY (CORRECT ANSWERS)

1.	C		11.	E
2.	D		12.	D
3.	A		13.	B
4.	B		14.	E
5.	E		15.	D
6.	C		16.	C
7.	A		17.	C
8.	A		18.	A
9.	E		19.	D
10.	E		20.	E

21.	D
22.	B
23.	E
24.	C
25.	D

TEST 2

DIRECTIONS: The following questions are designed to test your knowledge of grammar, sentence structure, correct usage, and punctuation. In each group, there is one sentence that contains an error. Select the letter of the INCORRECT sentence. *PRINT THE LETTER OF THE CORRECT ANSWER IN THE SPACE AT THE RIGHT.*

1.
   A. "Halt!" cried the sentry, "Who goes there?"
   B. "It is in talk alone," said Robert Louis Stevenson, "that we can learn our period and ourselves."
   C. The world will long remember the "culture" of the Nazis.
   D. When duty says, "You must," the youth replies, "I can."
   E. Who said, "Give me liberty or give me death?"

   1._____

2.
   A. Why are you so quiet, Martha?
   B. Edward Jones, a banker who lives near us, expects to retire very soon.
   C. I picked up the solid-gold chain.
   D. Any boy, who refuses to tell the truth, will be punished.
   E. Yes, honey tastes sweet.

   2._____

3.
   A. I knew it to be him by the style of his clothes.
   B. No one saw him doing it.
   C. Her going away is a loss to the community.
   D. Mary objected to her being there.
   E. Illness prevented him graduating in June.

   3._____

4.
   A. Being tired, I stretched out on a grassy knoll.
   B. While we were rowing on the lake, a sudden squall almost capsized the boat.
   C. Entering the room, a strange mark on the floor attracted my attention.
   D. Mounting the curb, the empty car crossed the sidewalk and came to rest against a building.
   E. Sitting down, they watched him demonstrate his skill.

   4._____

5.
   A. The coming of peace effected a change in her way of life.
   B. Spain is as weak, if not weaker than, she was in 1900.
   C. In regard to that, I am not certain what my attitude will be.
   D. That unfortunate family faces the problem of adjusting itself to a new way of life.
   E. Fred Eastman states in his essay that one of the joys of reading lies in discovering courage.

   5._____

6.
   A. Not one in a thousand readers take the matter seriously.
   B. Let it lie there.
   C. You are not as tall as he.
   D. The people began to realize how much she had done.
   E. He was able partially to accomplish his purpose.

   6._____

7. A. In the case of members who are absent, a special letter will be sent.
    B. The visitors were all ready to see it.
    C. I like Burns's poem "To a Mountain Daisy."
    D. John told William that he was sure he had seen it.
    E. Both men are Yale alumni.

8. A. The audience took their seats promptly.
    B. Each boy and girl must finish his examination this morning.
    C. Every person turned their eyes toward the door.
    D. Everyone has his own opinion.
    E. The club nominated its officers by secret ballot.

9. A. I can do that more easily than you.
    B. This kind of weather is more healthful.
    C. Pick out the really important points.
    D. Because of his aggressive nature, he only plays the hardest games.
    E. He pleaded with me to let him go.

10. A. It is I who am mistaken.
    B. Is it John or Susie who stand at the head of the class?
    C. He is one of those who always do their lessons.
    D. He is a man on whom I can depend in time of trouble.
    E. Had he known who it was, he would have come.

11. A. Somebody has forgotten his umbrella.
    B. Please let Joe and me use the car.
    C. We thought the author to be he.
    D. Whoever they send will be welcome.
    E. They thought the intruders were we.

12. A. If I had known that you were coming, I should have met you.
    B. All the girls but her were at the game.
    C. I expected to have heard the concert before the present time.
    D. Walter would not have said it if he had thought it would make her unhappy.
    E. I have always believed that cork is the best material for insulation.

13. A. Their contributions amounted to the no insignificant sum of ten thousand dollars.
    B. None of them was there.
    C. Ten dollars is the amount I agreed to pay.
    D. Fewer than one hundred persons assembled.
    E. Exactly what many others have done and are doing, Frank did.

14. A. Neither Jane or her sister has arrived.
    B. Either Richard or his brother is going to drive.
    C. Refilling storage batteries is the work of the youngest employee.
    D. Helen has to lie still for two weeks.
    E. Mother lay down for an hour yesterday.

15. A. He is not the man whom you saw entering the house.
    B. He asked why I wouldn't come.
    C. This is the cow whose horns are the longest.
    D. Helen, this is a man I met on the train one day last February.
    E. He greeted every foreign representative which came to the conference.

16. A. You, but not I, are invited.
    B. Guy's technique of service and return is masterly.
    C. Please pass me one of the books that are lying on the table.
    D. Mathematics is my most difficult subject.
    E. Unable to agree on a plan of organization, the class has departed in several directions.

17. A. He spoke to Gertrude and to me of the seriousness of the occasion.
    B. They seem to have decided to invite everyone except you and I.
    C. Your attitude is insulting to me who am your friend.
    D. He wished to know who our representative was.
    E. You may tell whomsoever you wish.

18. A. My favorite studies were Latin and science.
    B. The committee made its report.
    C. To get your work done promptly is better than leaving it until the last minute.
    D. That's what he would do if he were governor.
    E. He said that his chosen colors were red and blue.

19. A. Punish whoever disobeys orders.
    B. Come here, Henry; and sit with me.
    C. Has either of them his notebook?
    D. He talked as if he meant it.
    E. You did well; therefore you should be rewarded.

20. A. Many of us students were called to work.
    B. He shot the albatross with a crossbow.
    C. A house that is set on a hill is conspicuous.
    D. The wooden beams had raised slowly about a foot and then had settled back into place.
    E. Whom do you want to go with you?

21. A. He does not drive as he should.
    B. I can't hardly wait for the holidays.
    C. I like it less well than last week's.
    D. You were troubled by his coming.
    E. I don't know but that you are correct.

22. A. He was angry at both of us, her and me.
    B. When one enters the town, they see big crowds.
    C. They laid the tools on the ground every night.
    D. He is the only one of my friends who has written.
    E. He asked for a raise in wages.

23. A. None came with his excuse.
    B. Walking down the street, a house comes into view.
    C. "Never!" shouted the boy.
    D. Both are masters of their subject.
    E. His advice was to drive slowly.

24. A. There is both beef and lamb on the market.
    B. Either beans or beets are enough with potatoes.
    C. Where does your mother buy bananas?
    D. Dinners at the new restaurant are excellent.
    E. Each was rewarded according to his deeds.

25. A. Accordingly, we must prepare the food.
    B. The work, moreover, must be done today.
    C. Nevertheless, we must first have dinner.
    D. I always chose the most liveliest of the ponies.
    E. At six o'clock tomorrow the job will have been completed,

---

KEY (CORRECT ANSWERS)

1.	E	11.	C
2.	D	12.	C
3.	E	13.	A
4.	C	14.	A
5.	B	15.	E
6.	A	16.	E
7.	C	17.	B
8.	C	18.	C
9.	D	19.	B
10.	B	20.	D

21.	B
22.	B
23.	B
24.	A
25.	D

TEST 3

DIRECTIONS: In each group of five sentences below, one or more sentences contain an error in usage. Choose the lettered answer which indicates ALL the sentences containing errors in usage. *PRINT THE LETTER OF THE CORRECT ANSWER IN THE SPACE AT THE RIGHT.*

1.
   I. Shortly after the terms of the contract for the new road transpired, an aroused constituency showed its disapproval by voting the senator out of office.
   II. Neither father nor sons work for a living but spend their days in drinking and gambling at the pub.
   III. Like his Italian predecessor, Boccaccio, whose DECAMERON was used as a model, a company of people of various occupations and stations in life, brought together for a pilgrimage, are called upon to relate stories to help relieve the tedium of their journey,
   IV. Sarah hurried into the kitchen and after a half hour emerged with a nauseous brew which she called coffee.
   V. It was to the major that the people applied for redress and by his armed guards that they were driven away.

   The CORRECT answer is:
   A. I   B. III   C. I, II, III   D. IV, III   E. II, III

   1.____

2.
   I. As we approached the castle, which was illuminated suddenly by the full moon breaking through the clouds, we described a rider coming to meet us.
   II. The reason for his loss of interest in boxing, as far as I can see, was due to the pressure of his work and the distance of the local "Y" from his home.
   III. Accompanied by a handsome member of the British legation, Elsie was about to enter the luxuriously furnished salon to meet the countess.
   IV. In spite of all of John's gifts and attentions, little Rosalie, upon being asked to make a choice, said she liked me better than him.
   V. The scar of the clearing for the power line extended for a hundred miles over the mountains, and the great poles with fifty feet between each carried cable from Niagara to Albany.

   The CORRECT answer is:
   A. II, III   B. I, IV, III   C. I, II, IV, III
   D. II, V   E. III, V

   2.____

3.
   I. The high wind had blown the roofs of several houses; the water supply had been contaminated by the floods; transportation to the business center had ground to a half; but the mayor said there was no reason for alarm!
   II. Because there is a need to soften tragic or painful news, we resort to such euphuisms for the simple "to die" as "to pass away," "to go to a better world," or "to join the great majority."
   III. Hardly had the salient on the western shore of the river been obliterated than one on the eastern bank crossed on a pontoon bridge and in boats of all sorts.
   IV. The distinction between the man who gives in a spirit of charity and him who gives for social recognition is often to be seen in the nature of the gift.
   V. After a few months in office, the new superintendent effected many changes, not all of them for the good, in the administration of the plant.

   3.____

32

The CORRECT answer is:
A. II, III   B. II, III, IV   C. III, IV   D. I, II, V   E. I, II, III

4. I. The defendants published an advertisement and notice giving information, directly and indirectly, stating where, how, and when, and by what means and what purports to be the said book can be purchased.
    II. In common with most Eskimos of her time, she had long spells of silence; and nature, while endowing her with immense sagacity, had thrust on her a compelling reticence.
    III. The entire report was read in less than half an hour to the full committee, giving no time for comment or question, and offered for vote.
    IV. Students going through this course almost always find themselves becoming critical of their own writing.
    V. In his report of 1968, Mr. Jones states that his chief problem is the rapid turnover of personnel which has prevailed to the moment of writing.
    The CORRECT answer is:
    A. I, IV   B. II, III   C. III, IV, V   D. I, IV, V   E. I, III

4._____

5. I. The material was destroyed after it had served our purposes, and after portions of it had been excluded and portions included in our report.
    II. We checked our results very carefully, too carefully perhaps, for we spent several hours on our task.
    III. We should keep constantly in mind the fact that writing has no purpose save to meet the needs of the reader.
    IV. Not even discussed in October, when Lathrop flew in from the Coast, the problem of expense was settled at the June meeting.
    V. Whether our facts were right or not, it was not necessary for you to rebuke him in such a discourteous manner.
    The CORRECT answer is:
    A. I only   B. I, IV   C. II, III   D. V only   E. I, V

5._____

6. I. At first the novel was interesting and liked by members of the class; but later the long reading assignments dampened the pupils' enthusiasm.
    II. Donnie had no love or confidence in his mother, who, when abandoned by her husband, put the boy in an orphanage and seldom went to visit him.
    III. Built during the Civil War, the house has a delicate air, supported as it is by iron columns and rimmed by an iron railing.
    IV. Recently a newspaper editor from the South returned from an eight-week trip through the Caribbean and made a number of recommendations on what we should do to counter the lack of accurate information about the United States.
    V. The need is to be candid about our problems, to be informed on what we are going about them, and to resolve them as expeditiously as possible.
    The CORRECT answer is:
    A. I, II   B. II, III   C. III, IV   D. I, V   E. I, III

6._____

7. I. "Man is flying too fast for a world that is round," he said. "Soon he will catch up with himself in a great rear-end collision."
    II. After the raid on the club, each of the men suspected of accepting racetrack bets, along with the owner of the club, were held for questioning at police headquarters.
    III. It seems to me that at the opening performance of the play the audience were of different opinions about its merit and about its chances for a long run.
    IV. Oak from the forests of Vermont and steel from the mills of Pittsburgh are the material of this magnificent modern structure.
    V. The machine is subjected to severe strains which it must withstand and at the same time work easily and rapidly.
    The CORRECT answer is:
    A. I, II   B. II, III   C. IV, V   D. I, V   E. II, V

8. I. We don't have to worry about cutting down on expenses; money is no object in this venture.
    II. And now, my dear, let you and I tell our guests of the plans we have for the future.
    III. For all his errors of the past, no one can or has said that he did not turn out on this occasion a perfect piece of work.
    IV. Hercule Poirot, when looking for a suspect in the murder case never thought of its being me.
    V. During the interpellation the minister refused to answer any questions concerning his predecessor's conduct of the war.
    The CORRECT answer is:
    A. I, III   B. I, IV, V   C. II, III, IV   D. III, IV   E. II, III

9. I. John Steinbeck received the Nobel Prize only a few years ago for his work of the thirties, work, which now, according to some critics, has lost its timeliness and which never had timelessness.
    II. Respect is shown the flag by no matter when it is displayed, whether it be in the window of a private home or on the pole of a public building.
    III. When dinner was over we strolled through the garden and exclaimed at the beauty of the red gladioluses, the pride of the Jenkinses' gardener.
    IV. Mrs. Cosgrove's gift of $100,000 to the hospitals is only the latest of the many acts of generosity by which she has before now benefited her fellow men.
    V. Am I repeating your question exactly when I say, "How many of you are willing to join me in my attempt to rid America of the traitors who are threatening its freedom"?
    The CORRECT answer is:
    A. I, II, III, IV   B. II, IV   C. II, III, IV
    D. I, IV, V   E. I, II, IV

10. I. Slashing the original 73 projects to 20 with little loss of subject matter in the consolidated schedule, a stalemate was avoided and the work of the Council speeded up.

II. I was particularly struck by the unselfishness of the American school children, many of whom willingly donating their allowances, because they felt that they should help the refugees.
III. As a result of Henry VIII's defiance of the Church of Rome, the ecclesiastical principle of government was substituted by the national.
IV. I wish you had invited me to the concert, for I should have liked particularly to hear Piatigorsky.
V. John will be in the best possible position for getting the most out of his vacation and of making business contacts in new markets.
The CORRECT answer is:
A. I, II, III, IV   B. I, II, III, V   C. I, II, III
D. III, IV, V   E. I, II, III, IV, V

11. I. They took him to be me despite ever so many differences in our appearance and despite his addiction to loquacity.
II. They may have more money, they may have more possessions, but they are not any happier than us, as we and they all know.
III. Either Betty or Bob must have thought the teacher's remarks were addressed to him.
IV. There was present at today's conference—and at next week's conference the same group is expected—representatives of many foreign countries, including Italy, France, England, and Germany.
V. The most important criteria in judging the performance of a pianist is not virtuosity but maturity of interpretation.
The CORRECT answer is:
A. I, IV   B. II, III, V   C. II, IV, V   D. I, III   E. I, IV, V

12. I. Thoroughly exhausted after we had swum for six hours, we lay breathless on the sand and oblivious of anything but our utter fatigue.
II. The jury seems in violent disagreement about the culpability of the defendant; such shouting as we hear from the jury room is most unusual among these halls.
III. The difference between the class' average grades for the first week and those for the eighth week, on alternate forms of the same test, were quite insignificant, indicating, we thought, that instruction had been ineffective.
IV. Each tree and each bush give forth a flaming hue such as we have not seen for many seasons in these climes.
V. We met a man whom we thought we had met many years since, when we lived in South Africa.
The CORRECT answer is:
A. III, IV, V   B. I, II, V   C. III, IV   D. I, II   E. I, III, IV

13. I. That old friend, whom I met again last night after a lapse of many a year, stands head and shoulders above any person I have ever known.
II. This is one of the finest pictures which have ever been put on canvas, bringing out rare qualities of tone-color, mature interpretation, and virtuosity in execution.
III. Which of them would you prefer to have working for you, considering the inordinate physical and mental demands of the work, him or his brother?

IV. Throughout Saturday and Sunday, the townsfolk took scarcely any notice of the absence of Jed Gorman, believing him to be off on a drunken spree; but on Monday a body was discovered in the river obviously that of the missing handyman.
V. Things being so pleasant as they were, we could not fathom the reason for John leaving so soon after he had started what we considered an excellent job with unlimited opportunities.
The CORRECT answer is:
A. I, V   B. II, III, V   C. II, III   D. II, IV, V   E. I, IV, V

14.
I. He is unfailingly polite not only to his superiors and his colleagues but even to those who are in subordinate positions, and, in general, to whoever else he thinks is deserving of kindly consideration.
II. Without more ado, he took the books off the radiator, where they had lain quite neglected for several days and where their bindings were beginning to grow loose.
III. We can still include a discussion of the lunchroom situation among the topics, for the agenda have not yet been printed and will not be for another hour or two.
IV. We knew who would be at the party and who would take us home, but we didn't know who to expect to meet us at the station upon our arrival.
V. Despite his protestations, we know that the true reason why he was suffering such obvious anguish and failing to do his work was because of marital trouble.
The CORRECT answer is:
A. I, III, IV   B. II, III, V   C. I, IV, V   D. I, II   E. IV, V

15.
I. A difficult stretch of bad road in addition to a long detour which caused a series of minor motor mishaps, have much delayed our visitor's arrival and have created an awkward situation for us all.
II. To make the campaign effective, there is posted in every building, in full view of all entrants, one notice of the location of the shelter, and a second notice intended to boost morale and win cooperation.
III. One day while leading sheep in the desert and musing upon his people's future, the angel of the Lord appeared to Moses.
IV. Though he plead with the tongue of an angel, he will not ever alter her cold eyes nor trouble her calm fount of speech.
V. Despite continuous and well-advised and well-directed efforts by each of us, neither he nor I am able to improve the situation.
The CORRECT answer is:
A. I, V   B. III, IV, V   C. I, II, III   D. II, III, IV   E. I, III

16.
I. Though business has been brisk of late, this kind of appliances have not sold well at all, despite our continuous and concentrated efforts.
II. The return trip was a desperate one, with time of the essence; and partly blinded by the unexpected snowstorm, the trip was doubly hazardous.
III. I started on my journey by foot through forest and mountain, after a last warning to be careful about snake bites by my parents—a warning I knew I must heed on that dangerous terrain.

IV. That he was losing to a better man, a man who had worked diligently and a man of impeccable virtue, was a consideration of but small import to him.
V. The precarious state of affairs was aggravated by a new hazard, notwithstanding all our cautions to avoid any change in the situation.
The CORRECT answer is:
A. I, III, V   B. II, IV   C. IV, V   D. I, II, III   E. II, III

17. I. Who's responsible for the feeding of his cat and its young, I'd like to know, we or they? If we, let's feed them.
II. The books that had lain on the desk for many weeks were laid in the bookcase, where they lay until picked up by the messenger from the second-handbook shop.
III. You say I merit the award for competence in my duties; but he deserves an award as well as I, for he is as good, without doubt, or even better than I.
IV. The Joneses' car was more luxurious than, but not necessarily as expensive as, the Browns'.
V. Slowly they tiptoed into the living room hoping not to be heard, but we were fully aware of it being they.
The CORRECT answer is:
A. II, IV   B. I, III, IV   C. I, V   D. I, II, V   E. III, V

18. I. I shall lay the rug in the sun, where it has laid many times before; and I shall lie in the sun, too, as always I have lain at leisure while the rug has been drying.
II. Though he knew a great deal about printing machinery, he thought, mistakenly, that the new machine could be made to cast type as well as setting it up.
III. Knowledge in several major fields with sympathy for varied points of view make him an excellent choice for student adviser.
IV. You will find the girls' equipment in the teachers' lounge where the boy's father left it at Professor Wills's suggestion.
V. I know that the Burnses have worked for the mill for generations, and that the Smiths have but recently removed from town, but does either of the Norton boys work here?
The CORRECT answer is:
A. I, II, III   B. II, III, IV   C. I, IV, V   D. III, V   E. I, II, IV

19. I. I can put two and two together as quick as most mean; but understanding how he, a slow-witted dolt, could achieve so notable a victory over his opponent is one of the things that puzzle and, forevermore, will puzzle me.
II. Besides my two brothers, my sister, and I, there are a cousin and my father's nephew living at home with us,
III. He has lived in the Reno for many years; previously he lived in Chicago for a short space, after he had come from Los Angeles.
IV. Researchers have been baffled for a long time by this statistic, for it contradicts many of their most highly cherished hypotheses.
V. So intense was the heat near the furnace that all the men at work could not carry on; consequently, production came to a halt,

The CORRECT answer is:
A. I, II, IV B. III, V C. I, III, IV D. I, II, V E. II, V

20. I. If we can escape from our desks for a brief interval, let's you, Henry, and I put in an appearance at the party.
    II. If you persevere in your ambitions, you are likely to achieve at least a modicum of success; if you malinger, you are liable to court failure.
    III. You may find conditions here congenial, but since I neither like he work nor the salary, it is to no avail for you to attempt to persuade me to stay.
    IV. He has never deigned to take a drink with us, his office colleagues, though we know him now for over fifteen years; and he takes an occasional drink, we know, at home and at his golf club,
    V. Though the results of your investigation are at variance with the hypothesis we advanced, I believe you have interpreted these data in the only ways that have scientific validity.
    The CORRECT answer is:
    A. I, II, IV B. I, II C. IV, V D. II, III, V E. I, III, IV

21. I. He can't hardly hear anything unless the room is completely quiet.
    II. His attitude seemed perfectly alright to me.
    III. One can't be too careful, can one?
    IV. He is one of those people who believe in the perfectability of man.
    V. His uneasiness is reflected in his unwillingness to compromise on even the smallest point.
    The CORRECT answer is:
    A. II, III, V B. I, III C. I, IV, V D. I, II, IV E. III, IV

22. I. "Have you found what you were looking for?" he asked.
    II. "I have never," she insisted, "Seen such careless disregard for the rights of others."
    III. "I found this ticket on the step," he said. "Did you lose it?"
    IV. "In one way I'd like to enter the contest," said Anne; "in another way I'm not too eager."
    V. "Did he say, 'I'm coming?'"
    The CORRECT answer is:
    A. I, III, IV B. II, V C. III, V D. II, IV E. I, II, IV

23. I. Were I the owner of the dog, I'd keep him muzzled.
    II. In the tennis match Don was paired with Bill; Ed, with Al.
    III. He was given an excellent trade-in allowance on his old car.
    IV. Why doesn't this window raise?
    V. The prow of the vessel had almost completely sank by the time the rescuers arrived on the scene.
    The CORRECT answer is:
    A. I, II, V B. I, IV, V C. I, II, III D. II, V E. IV, V

24.
   I. Turning the pages rapidly, his glance fell upon a peculiarly worded advertisement.
   II. Turning the pages rapidly, his eyes noticed a peculiarly worded advertisement.
   III. Turning the pages rapidly, he noticed a peculiarly worded advertisement.
   IV. Turning the pages rapidly made him more attentive to the unusual.
   V. Turning the pages rapidly does not guarantee rapid comprehension.
   The CORRECT answer is:
   A. III, IV, V   B. I, II, IV   C. III, V   D. I, II   E. I, II, III

25.
   I. They told us how they had suffered.
   II. It is interesting (a) to the student, (b) to the parent, and (c) to the teacher.
   III. There were blue, green and red banners.
   IV. "Will you help", he asked?
   V. In addition to reproducibility, an attitude scale must meet various other requirements characteristic of scale analysis procedures.
   The CORRECT answer is:
   A. I, II   B. II, III   C. I only   D. IV only   E. IV, V

KEY (CORRECT ANSWERS)

1.	C		11.	C
2.	D		12.	C
3.	A		13.	D
4.	E		14.	E
5.	A		15.	C
6.	A		16.	D
7.	E		17.	C
8.	A		18.	A
9.	B		19.	E
10.	B		20.	F

21. D
22. B
23. E
24. D
25. D

EXAMINATION SECTION
TEST 1

DIRECTIONS: In each of the following questions, only one of the four sentences conforms to standards of correct usage. The other three contain errors in grammar, diction, or punctuation. Select the choice in each question which BEST conforms to standards of correct usage. Consider a choice correct if it contains none of the errors mentioned above, even though there may be other ways of expressing the same thought. *PRINT THE LETTER OF THE CORRECT ANSWER IN THE SPACE AT THE RIGHT.*

1. A. Because he was ill was no excuse for his behavior
   B. I insist that he see a lawyer before he goes to trial.
   C. He said "that he had not intended to go."
   D. He wasn't out of the office only three days.

   1._____

2. A. He came to the station and pays a porter to carry his bags into the train.
   B. I should have liked to live in medieval times.
   C. My father was born in Linville. A little country town where everybody knows everyone else.
   D. The car, which is parked across the street, is disabled.

   2._____

3. A. He asked the desk clerk for a clean, quiet, room.
   B. I expected James to be lonesome and that he would want to go home.
   C. I have stopped worrying because I have heard nothing further on the subject.
   D. If the board of directors controls the company, they may take actions which are disapproved by the stockholders.

   3._____

4. A. Each of the players knew their place.
   B. He whom you saw on the stage is the son of an actor.
   C. Susan is the smartest of the twin sisters.
   D. Who ever thought of him winning both prizes?

   4._____

5. A. An outstanding trait of early man was their reliance on omens.
   B. Because I had never been there before.
   C. Neither Mr. Jones nor Mr. Smith has completed his work.
   D. While eating my dinner, a dog came to the window.

   5._____

6. A. A copy of the lease, in addition to the Rules and Regulations, are to be given to each tenant.
   B. The Rules and Regulations and a copy of the lease is being given to each tenant.
   C. A copy of the lease, in addition to the Rules and Regulations, is to be given to each tenant.
   D. A copy of the lease, in addition to the Rules and Regulations, are being given to each tenant.

   6._____

7.
   A. Although we understood that for him music was a passion, we were disturbed by the fact that he was addicted to sing along with the soloists.
   B. Do you believe that Steven is liable to win a scholarship?
   C. Give the picture to whomever is a connoisseur of art.
   D. Whom do you believe to be the most efficient worker in the office?

7._____

8.
   A. Each adult who is sure they know all the answers will some day realize their mistake.
   B. Even the most hardhearted villain would have to feel bad about so horrible a tragedy.
   C. Neither being licensed teachers, both aspirants had to pass rigorous tests before being appointed.
   D. The principal reason why he wanted to be designated was because he had never before been to a convention.

8._____

9.
   A. Being that the weather was so inclement, the party has been postponed for at least a month.
   B. He is in New York City only three weeks and he has already seen all the thrilling sights in Manhattan and in the other four boroughs.
   C. If you will look it up in the official directory, which can be consulted in the library during specified hours, you will discover that the chairman and director are Mr. T. Henry Long.
   D. Working hard at college during the day and at the post office during the night, he appeared to his family to be indefatigable.

9._____

10.
   A. I would have been happy to oblige you if you only asked me to do it.
   B. The cold weather, as well as the unceasing wind and rain, have made us decide to spend the winter in Florida.
   C. The politician would have been more successful in winning office if he would have been less dogmatic.
   D. These trousers are expensive; however, they will wear well.

10._____

11.
   A. All except him wore formal attire at the reception for the ambassador.
   B. If that chair were to be blown off of the balcony, it might injure someone below.
   C. Not a passenger, who was in the crash, survived the impact.
   D. To borrow money off friends is the best way to lose them.

11._____

12.
   A. Approaching Manhattan on the ferry boat from Staten Island, an unforgettable sight of the skyscrapers is seen.
   B. Did you see the exhibit of modernistic paintings as yet?
   C. Gesticulating wildly and ranting in stentorian tones, the speaker was the sinecure of all eyes.
   D. The airplane with crew and passengers was lost somewhere in the Pacific Ocean.

12._____

13. A. If one has consistently had that kind of training, it is certainly too late to change your entire method of swimming long distances.
     B. The captain would have been more impressed if you would have been more conscientious in evacuation drills.
     C. The passengers on the stricken ship were all ready to abandon it at the signal.
     D. The villainous shark lashed at the lifeboat with it's tail, trying to upset the rocking boat in order to partake of it's contents.

13.____

14. A. As one whose been certified as a professional engineer, I believe that the decision to build a bridge over that harbor is unsound.
     B. Between you and me, this project ought to be completed long before winter arrives.
     C. He fervently hoped that the men would be back at camp and to find them busy at their usual chores.
     D. Much to his surprise, he discovered that the climate of Korea was like his home town.

14.____

15. A. An industrious executive is aided, not impeded, by having a hobby which gives him a fresh point of view on life and its problems.
     B. Frequent absence during the calendar year will surely mitigate against the chances of promotion.
     C. He was unable to go to the committee meeting because he was very ill.
     D. Mr. Brown expressed his disapproval so emphatically that his associates were embarassed

15.____

16. A. At our next session, the office manager will have told you something about his duties and responsibilities.
     B. In general, the book is absorbing and original and have no hesitation about recommending it.
     C. The procedures followed by private industry in dealing with lateness and absence are different from ours.
     D We shall treat confidentially any information about Mr. Doe, to whom we understand you have sent reports to for many years.

16.____

17. A. I talked to one official, whom I knew was fully impartial.
     B. Everyone signed the petition but him.
     C. He proved not only to be a good student but also a good athlete.
     D. All are incorrect.

17.____

18. A. Every year a large amount of tenants are admitted to housing projects.
     B. Henry Ford owned around a billion dollars in industrial equipment.
     C. He was aggravated by the child's poor behavior.
     D. All are incorrect.

18.____

19. A. Before he was committed to the asylum he suffered from the illusion that he was Napoleon. 19.____
    B. Besides stocks, there were also bonds in the safe.
    C. We bet the other team easily.
    D. All are incorrect.

20. A. Bring this report to your supervisory. 20.____
    B. He set the chair down near the table.
    C. The capitol of New York is Albany.
    D. All are incorrect.

21. A. He was chosen to arbitrate the dispute because everyone knew he would be disinterested. 21.____
    B. It is advisable to obtain the best council before making an important decision.
    C. Less college students are interested in teaching than ever before.
    D. All are incorrect.

22. A. She, hearing a signal, the source lamp flashed. 22.____
    B. While hearing a signal, the source lamp flashed.
    C. In hearing a signal, the source lamp flashed.
    D. As she heard a signal, the source lamp flashed.

23. A. Every one of the time records have been initialed in the designated spaces. 23.____
    B. All of the time records has been initialed in the designated spaces.
    C. Each one of the time records was initialed in the designated spaces.
    D. The time records all been initialed in the designated spaces.

24. A. If there is no one else to answer the phone, you will have to answer it. 24.____
    B. You will have to answer it yourself if no one else answers the phone.
    C. If no one else is not around to pick up the phone, you will have to do it.
    D. You will have to answer the phone when nobodys here to do it.

25. A. Dr. Barnes not in his office. What could I do for you? 25.____
    B. Dr. Barnes is not in his office. Is there something I can do for you?
    C. Since Dr. Barnes is not in his office, might there be something I may do for you?
    D. Is there any ways I can assist you since Dr. Barnes is not in his office?

26. A. She do not understand how the new console works. 26.____
    B. The way the new console works, she doesn't understand.
    C. She doesn't understand how the new console works.
    D. The new console works, so that she doesn't understand.

27. A. Certain changes in my family income must be reported as they occur. 27.____
    B. When certain changes in family income occur, it must be reported.
    C. Certain family income change must be reported as they occur.
    D. Certain changes in family income must be reported as they have been occurring.

28. A. Each tenant has to complete the application themselves.
    B. Each of the tenants have to complete the application by himself.
    C. Each of the tenants has to complete the application himself.
    D. Each of the tenants has to complete the application by themselves.

28.____

29. A. Yours is the only building that the construction will effect.
    B. Your's is the only building affected by the construction.
    C. The construction will only effect your building.
    D. Yours is the only building that will be affected by the construction.

29.____

30. A. There is four tests left.
    B. The number of tests left are four.
    C. There are four tests left.
    D. Four of the tests remains.

30.____

31. A. Each of the applicants takes a test.
    B. Each of the applicant take a test.
    C. Each of the applicants take tests.
    D. Each of the applicants have taken tests.

31.____

32. A. The applicant, not the examiners, are ready.
    B. The applicants, not the examiners, is ready.
    C. The applicants, not the examiner, are ready.
    D. The applicant, not the examiner, are ready

32.____

33. A. You will not progress except you practice.
    B. You will not progress without you practicing.
    C. You will not progress unless you practice.
    D. You will not progress provided you do not practice.

33.____

34. A. Neither the director or the employees will be at the office tomorrow.
    B. Neither the director nor the employees will be at the office tomorrow.
    C. Neither the director, or the secretary nor the other employees will be at the office tomorrow.
    D. Neither the director, the secretary or the other employees will be at the office tomorrow.

34.____

35. A. In my absence, he and her will have to finish the assignment.
    B. In my absence he and she will have to finish the assignment.
    C. In my absence she and him, they will have to finish the assignment.
    D. In my absence he and her both will have to finish the assignment.

35.____

KEY (CORRECT ANSWERS)

1. B	11. A	21. A	31. A
2. B	12. D	22. D	32. C
3. C	13. C	23. C	33. C
4. B	14. B	24. A	34. B
5. C	15. A	25. B	35. B
6. C	16. C	26. C	
7. D	17. B	27. A	
8. B	18. D	28. C	
9. D	19. B	29. D	
10. D	20. B	30. C	

TEST 2

DIRECTIONS: Each question or incomplete statement is followed by several suggested answers or completions. Select the one that BEST answers the question or completes the statement. *PRINT THE LETTER OF THE CORRECT ANSWER IN THE SPACE AT THE RIGHT.*

Questions 1-4.

DIRECTIONS: Questions 1 through 4 consist of three sentences each. For each question, select the sentence which contains NO error in grammar or usage.

1. A. Be sure that everybody brings his notes to the conference. 1.____
    B. He looked like he meant to hit the boy.
    C. Mr. Jones is one of the clients who was chosen to represent the district.
    D. All are incorrect.

2. A. He is taller than I. 2.____
    B. I'll have nothing to do with these kind of people.
    C. The reason why he will not buy the house is because it is too expensive.
    D. All are incorrect.

3. A. Aren't I eligible for this apartment. 3.____
    B. Have you seen him anywheres?
    C. He should of come earlier.
    D. All are incorrect.

4. A. He graduated college in 2022. 4.____
    B. He hadn't but one more line to write.
    C. Who do you think is the author of this report?
    D. All are incorrect.

Questions 5-35.

DIRECTIONS: In each of the following questions, only one of the four sentences conforms to standards of correct usage. The other three contain errors in grammar, diction, or punctuation. Select the choice in each question which BEST conforms to standards of correct usage. Consider a choice correct if it contains none of the errors mentioned above, even though there may be other ways of expressing the same thought.

5. A. It is obvious that no one wants to be a kill-joy if they can help it. 5.____
    B. It is not always possible, and perhaps it never ispossible, to judge a person's character by just looking at him.
    C. When Yogi Berra of the New York Yankees hit an immortal grandslam home run, everybody in the huge stadium including Pittsburgh fans, rose to his feet.
    D. Every one of us students must pay tuition today.

6. A. The physician told the young mother that if the baby is not able to digest its milk, it should be boiled.
   B. There is no doubt whatsoever that he felt deeply hurt because John Smith had betrayed the trust.
   C. Having partaken of a most delicious repast prepared by Tessie Breen, the hostess, the horses were driven home immediately thereafter.
   D. The attorney asked my wife and myself several questions.

6._____

7. A. Despite all denials, there is no doubt in my mind that
   B. At this time everyone must deprecate the demogogic attack made by one of our Senators on one of our most revered statesmen.
   C. In the first game of a crucial two-game series, Ted Williams, got two singles, both of them driving in a run.
   D. Our visitor brought good news to John and I.

7._____

8. A. If he would have told me, I should have been glad to help him in his dire financial emergency.
   B. Newspaper men have often asserted that diplomats or so-called official spokesmen sometimes employ equivocation in attempts to deceive.
   C. I think someones coming to collect money for the Red Cross.
   D. In a masterly summation, the young attorney expressed his belief that the facts clearly militate against this opinion.

8._____

9. A. We have seen most all the exhibits.
   B. Without in the least underestimating your advice, in my opinion the situation has grown immeasurably worse in the past few days.
   C. I wrote to the box office treasurer of the hit show that a pair of orchestra seats would be preferable.
   D. As the grim story of Pearl Harbor was broadcast on that fateful December 7, it was the general opinion that war was inevitable.

9._____

10. A. Without a moment's hesitation, Casey Stengel said that Larry Berra works harder than any player on the team.
    B. There is ample evidence to indicate that many animals can run faster than any human being.
    C. No one saw the accident but I.
    D. Example of courage is the heroic defense put up by the paratroopers against overwhelming odds.

10._____

11. A. If you prefer these kind, Mrs. Grey, we shall be more than willing to let you have them reasonably.
    B. If you like these here, Mrs. Grey, we shall be more than willing to let you have them reasonably.
    C. If you like these, Mrs. Grey, we shall be more than willing to let you have them.
    D. Who shall we appoint?

11._____

12. A. The number of errors are greater in speech than in writing.
     B. The doctor rather than the nurse was to blame for his being neglected.
     C. Because the demand for these books have been so great, we reduced the price.
     D. John Galsworthy, the English novelist, could not have survived a serious illness; had it not been for loving care.

13. A. Our activities this year have seldom ever been as interesting as they have been this month.
     B. Our activities this month have been more interesting, or at least as interesting as those of any month this year.
     C. Our activities this month has been more interesting than those of any other month this year.
     D. Neither Jean nor her sister was at home.

14. A. George B. Shaw's view of common morality, as well as his wit sparkling with a dash of perverse humor here and there, have led critics to term him "The Incurable Rebel."
     B. The President's program was not always received with the wholehearted endorsement of his own party, which is why the party faces difficulty in drawing up a platform for the coming election.
     C. The reason why they wanted to travel was because they had never been away from home.
     D. Facing a barrage of cameras, the visiting celebrity found it extremely difficult to express his opinions clearly.

15. A. When we calmed down, we all agreed that our anger had been kind of unnecessary and had not helped the situation.
     B. Without him going into all the details, he made us realize the horror of the accident.
     C. Like one girl, for example, who applied for two positions.
     D. Do not think that you have to be so talented as he is in order to play in the school orchestra.

16. A. He looked very peculiarly to me.
     B. He certainly looked at me peculiar.
     C. Due to the train's being late, we had to wait an hour.
     D. The reason for the poor attendance is that it is raining.

17. A. About one out of four own an automobile.
     B. The collapse of the old Mitchell Bridge was caused by defective construction in the central pier.
     C. Brooks Atkinson was well acquainted with the best literature, thus helping him to become an able critic.
     D. He has to stand still until the relief man comes up, thus giving him no chance to move about and keep warm.

18. A. He is sensitive to confusion and withdraws from people whom he feels are too noisy.
    B. Do you know whether the data is statistically correct?
    C. Neither the mayor or the aldermen are to blame.
    D. Of those who were graduated from high school, a goodly percentage went to college.

18.____

19. A. Acting on orders, the offices were searched by a designated committee.
    B. The answer probably is nothing.
    C. I thought it to be all right to excuse them from class.
    D. I think that he is as successful a singer, if not more successful, than Mary.

19.____

20. A. $360,000 is really very little to pay for such a wellbuilt house.
    B. The creatures looked like they had come from outer space.
    C. It was her, he knew!
    D. Nobody but me knows what to do.

20.____

21. A. Mrs. Smith looked good in her new suit.
    B. New York may be compared with Chicago.
    C. I will not go to the meeting except you go with me.
    D. I agree with this editorial.

21.____

22. A. My opinions are different from his.
    B. There will be less students in class now.
    C. Helen was real glad to find her watch.
    D. It had been pushed off of her dresser.

22.____

23. A. Almost everyone, who has been to California, returns with glowing reports.
    B. George Washington, John Adams, and Thomas Jefferson, were our first presidents.
    C. Mr. Walters, whom we met at the bank yesterday, is the man, who gave me my first job.
    D. One should study his lessons as carefully as he can.

23.____

24. A. We had such a good time yesterday.
    B. When the bell rang, the boys and girls went in the schoolhouse.
    C. John had the worst headache when he got up this morning.
    D. Today's assignment is somewhat longer than yesterday's.

24.____

25. A. Neither the mayor nor the city clerk are willing to talk.
    B. Neither the mayor nor the city clerk is willing to talk.
    C. Neither the mayor or the city clerk are willing to talk.
    D Neither the mayor or the city clerk is willing to talk.

25.____

26. A. Being that he is that kind of boy, cooperation cannot be expected.
    B. He interviewed people who he thought had something to say.
    C. Stop whomever enters the building regardless of rank or office held.
    D. Passing through the countryside, the scenery pleased us.

26.____

27. A. The childrens' shoes were in their closet. 27.____
    B. The children's shoes were in their closet.
    C. The childs' shoes were in their closet.
    D. The childs' shoes were in his closet.

28. A. An agreement was reached between the defendant, the plaintiff, the 28.____
       plaintiff's attorney and the insurance company as to the amount of the
       settlement.
    B. Everybody was asked to give their versions of the accident.
    C. The consensus of opinion was that the evidence was inconclusive.
    D. The witness stated that if he was rich, he wouldn't have had to loan the
       money.

29. A. Before beginning the investigation, all the materials related to the case were 29.____
       carefully assembled.
    B. The reason for his inability to keep the appointment is because of his injury
       in the accident.
    C. This here evidence tends to support the claim of the defendant.
    D. We interviewed all the witnesses who, according to the driver, were still in
       town.

30. A. Each claimant was allowed the full amount of their medical expenses. 30.____
    B. Either of the three witnesses is available.
    C. Every one of the witnesses was asked to tell his story.
    D. Neither of the witnesses are right.

31. A. The commissioner, as well as his deputy and various bureau heads, were 31.____
       present.
    B. A new organization of employers and employees have been formed.
    C. One or the other of these men have been selected.
    D. The number of pages in the book is enough to discourage a reader.

32. A. Between you and me, I think he is the better man. 32.____
    B. He was believed to be me.
    C. Is it us that you wish to see?
    D. The winners are him and her.

33. A. Beside the statement to the police, the witness spoke to no one. 33.____
    B. He made no statement other than to the police and I.
    C. He made no statement to any one else, aside from the police.
    D. The witness spoke to no one but me.

34. A. The claimant has no one to blame but himself. 34.____
    B. The boss sent us, he and I, to deliver the packages.
    C. The lights come from mine and not his car.
    D. There was room on the stairs for him and myself.

35.	A. Admission to this clinic is limited to patients' inability to pay for medical care.
	B. Patients who can pay little or nothing for medical care are treated in this clinic.
	C. The patient's ability to pay for medical care is the determining factor in his admission to this clinic.
	D. This clinic is for the patient's that cannot afford to pay or that can pay a little for medical care.

35._____

KEY (CORRECT ANSWERS)

1.	A	11.	C	21.	A	31.	D
2.	A	12.	B	22.	A	32.	A
3.	D	13.	D	23.	D	33.	D
4.	C	14.	D	24.	D	34.	A
5.	D	15.	D	25.	B	35.	B
6.	D	16.	D	26.	B		
7.	B	17.	B	27.	B		
8.	B	18.	D	28.	C		
9.	D	19.	B	29.	D		
10.	B	20.	D	30.	C		

EXAMINATION SECTION
TEST 1

DIRECTIONS: Each question or incomplete statement is followed by several suggested answers or completions. Select the one that BEST answers the question or completes the statement. *PRINT THE LETTER OF THE CORRECT ANSWER IN THE SPACE AT THE RIGHT.*

1. Which of the following sentences is punctuated INCORRECTLY?　　　　　　　　1._____
   A. Johnson said, "One tiny virus, Blanche, can multiply so fast that it will become 200 viruses in 25 minutes."
   B. With economic pressures hitting them from all sides, American farmers have become the weak link in the food chain.
   C. The degree to which this is true, of course, depends on the personalities of the people involved, the subject matter, and the atmosphere in general.
   D. "What loneliness, asked George Eliot, is more lonely than distrust?"

2. Which of the following sentences is punctuated INCORRECTLY?　　　　　　　　2._____
   A. Based on past experiences, do you expect the plumber to show up late, not have the right parts, and overcharge you.
   B. When polled, however, the participants were most concerned that it be convenient.
   C. No one mentioned the flavor of the coffee, and no one seemed to care that china was used instead of plastic.
   D. As we said before, sometimes people view others as things; they don't see them as living, breathing beings like themselves.

3. Convention members travelled here from Kingston New York Pittsfield　　　　　3._____
   Massachusetts Bennington Vermont and Hartford Connecticut.
   How many commas should there be in the above sentence?
   A. 3　　　　　B. 4　　　　　C. 5　　　　　D. 6

4. Of the two speakers the one who spoke about human rights is more famous　　　4._____
   and more humble.
   How many commas should there be in the above sentence?
   A. 1　　　　　B. 2　　　　　C. 3　　　　　D. 4

5. Which sentence is punctuated INCORRECTLY?　　　　　　　　　　　　　　　　5._____
   A. Five people voted no; two voted yes; one person abstained.
   B. Well, consider what has been said here today, but we won't make any promises.
   C. Anthropologists divide history into three major periods: the Stone Age, the Bronze Age, and the Iron Age.
   D. Therefore, we may create a stereotype about people who are unsuccessful; we may see them as lazy, unintelligent, or afraid of success.

6. Which sentence is punctuated INCORRECTLY?
   A. Studies have found that the unpredictability of customer behavior can lead to a great deal of stress, particularly if the behavior is unpleasant or if the employee has little control over it.
   B. If this degree of emotion and variation can occur in spectator sports, imagine the role that perceptions can play when there are <u>real</u> stakes involved.
   C. At other times, however hidden expectations may sabotage or severely damage an encounter without anyone knowing what happened.
   D. There are usually four issues to look for in a conflict: differences in values, goals, methods, and facts.

6._____

Questions 7-10.

DIRECTIONS: Questions 7 through 10 test your ability to distinguish between words that sound alike but are spelled differently and have different meanings. In the following groups of sentences, one of the underlined words is used incorrectly.

7. A. By <u>accepting</u> responsibility for their actions, managers promote trust.
   B. Dropping hints or making <u>illusions</u> to things that you would like changed sometimes leads to resentment.
   C. The entire unit <u>loses</u> respect for the manager and resents the reprimand.
   D. Many people are <u>averse</u> to confronting problems directly; they would rather avoid them.

7._____

8. A. What does this say about the <u>effect</u> our expectations have on those we supervise?
   B. In an effort to save time between 9 A.M. and 1 P.M., the staff members devised <u>their</u> own interpretation of what was to be done on these forms.
   C. The taskmaster's <u>principal</u> concern is for getting the work done; he or she is not concerned about the need or interests of employees.
   D. The advisor's main objective was increasing Angela's ability to invest her <u>capitol</u> wisely.

8._____

9. A. A typical problem is that people have to cope with the internal <u>censer</u> of their feelings.
   B. Sometimes, in their attempt to sound more learned, people speak in ways that are barely <u>comprehensible</u>.
   C. The <u>council</u> will meet next Friday to decide whether Abrams should continue as representative.
   D. His <u>descent</u> from grace was assured by that final word.

9._____

10. A. The doctor said that John's leg had to remain <u>stationary</u> or it would not heal properly.
    B. There is a city <u>ordinance</u> against parking too close to fire hydrants.
    C. Meyer's problem is that he is never <u>discrete</u> when talking about office politics.
    D. Mrs. Thatcher probably worked harder <u>than</u> any other British Prime Minister had ever worked.

10._____

3 (#1)

Questions 11-20.

DIRECTIONS: For each of the following groups of sentences in Questions 11 through 20, select the sentence which is the BEST example of English usage and grammar.

11. A. She is a woman who, at age sixty, is distinctly attractive and cares about how they look.
    B. It was a seemingly impossible search, and no one knew the problems better than she.
    C. On the surface, they are all sweetness and light, but his morbid character is under it.
    D. The minicopier, designed to appeal to those who do business on the run like architects in the field or business travelers, weigh about four pounds.

11._____

12. A. Neither the administrators nor the union representative regret the decision to settle the disagreement.
    B. The plans which are made earlier this year were no longer being considered.
    C. I would have rode with him if I had known he was leaving at five.
    D. I don't know who she said had it.

12._____

13. A. Writing at a desk, the memo was handed to her for immediate attention.
    B. Carla didn't water Carl's plants this week, which she never does.
    C. Not only are they good workers, with excellent writing and speaking skills, and they get to the crux of any problem we hand them.
    D. We've noticed that this enthusiasm for undertaking new projects sometimes interferes with his attention to detail.

13._____

14. A. It's obvious that Nick offends people by being unruly, inattentive, and having no patience.
    B. Marcia told Genie that she would have to leave soon.
    C. Here are the papers you need to complete your investigation.
    D. Julio was startled by you're comment.

14._____

15. A. The new manager has done good since receiving her promotion, but her secretary has helped her a great deal.
    B. One of the personnel managers approached John and tells him that the client arrived unexpectedly.
    C. If somebody can supply us with the correct figures, they should do so immediately.
    D. Like zealots, advocates seek power because they want to influence the policies and actions of an organization.

15._____

16. A. Between you and me, Chris probably won't finish this assignment in time.
    B. Rounding the corner, the snack bar appeared before us.
    C. Parker's radical reputation made to the Supreme Court his appointment impossible.
    D. By the time we arrived, Marion finishes briefing James and returns to Hank's office.

    16.___

17. A. As we pointed out earlier, the critical determinant of the success of middle managers is their ability to communicate well with others.
    B. The lecturer stated there wasn't no reason for bad supervision.
    C. We are well aware whose at fault in this instance.
    D. When planning important changes, it's often wise to seek the participation of others because employees often have much valuable ideas to offer.

    17.___

18. A. Joan had ought to throw out those old things that were damaged when the roof leaked.
    B. I spose he'll let us know what he's decided when he finally comes to a decision.
    C. Carmen was walking to work when she suddenly realized that she had left her lunch on the table as she passed the market.
    D. Are these enough plants for your new office?

    18.___

19. A. First move the lever forward, and then they should lift the ribbon casing before trying to take it out.
    B. Michael finished quickest than any other person in the office.
    C. There is a special meeting for we committee members today at 4 p.m.
    D. My husband is worried about our having to work overtime next week.

    19.___

20. A. Another source of conflicts are individuals who possess very poor interpersonal skills.
    B. It is difficult for us to work with him on projects because these kinds of people are not interested in team building.
    C. Each of the departments was represented at the meeting.
    D. Poor boy, he never should of past that truck on the right.

    20.___

Questions 21-28.

DIRECTIONS: In Questions 21 through 28, there may be a problem with English grammar or usage. If a problem does exist, select the letter that indicates the most effective change. If no problem exists, select Choice A.

21. He rushed her to the hospital and stayed with her, even though this took quite a bit of his time, he didn't charge her anything.
    A. No changes are necessary.
    B. Change even though to although
    C. Change the first comma to a period and capitalize even
    D. Change rushed to had rushed

    21.___

22. Waiting that appears unfairly feels longer than waiting that seems justified. 22._____
    A. No changes are necessary.
    B. Change unfairly to unfair
    C. Change appears to seems
    D. Change longer to longest

23. May be you and the person who argued with you will be able to reach an agreement. 23._____
    A. No changes are necessary
    B. Change will be to were
    C. Change argued with to had an argument with
    D. Change May be to Maybe

24. Any one of them could of taken the file while you were having coffee. 24._____
    A. No changes are necessary
    B. Change any one to anyone
    C. Change of to have
    D. Change were having to were out having

25. While people get jobs or move from poverty level to better paying employment, they stop receiving benefits and start paying taxes. 25._____
    A. No changes are necessary
    B. Change While to As
    C. Change stop to will stop
    D. Change get to obtain

26. Maribeth's phone rang while talking to George about the possibility of their meeting Tom at three this afternoon. 26._____
    A. No changes are necessary
    B. Change their to her
    C. Move to George so that it follows Tom
    D. Change talking to she was talking

27. According to their father, Lisa is smarter than Chris, but Emily is the smartest of the three sisters. 27._____
    A. No changes are necessary
    B. Change their to her
    C. Change is to was
    D. Make two sentences, changing the second comma to a period and omitting but

28. Yesterday, Mark and he claim that Carl took Carol's ideas and used them inappropriately. 28._____
    A. No changes are necessary
    B. Change claim to claimed
    C. Change inappropriately to inappropriate
    D. Change Carol's to Carols'

Questions 29-34.

DIRECTIONS: For each group of sentences in Questions 29 through 34, select the choice that represents the BEST editing of the problem sentence.

29. The managers expected employees to be at their desks at all times, but they would always be late or leave unannounced.
    A. The managers wanted employees to always be at their desks, but they would always be late or leave unannounced.
    B. Although the managers expected employees to be at their desks no matter what came up, they would always be late and leave without telling anyone.
    C. Although the managers expected employees to be at their desks at all times, the managers would always be late or leave without telling anyone.
    D. The managers expected the employee to never leave their desks, but they would always be late or leave without telling anyone.

30. The one who is department manager he will call you to discuss the problem tomorrow morning at 10 A.M.
    A. The one who is department manager will call you tomorrow morning at ten to discuss the problem.
    B. The department manager will call you to discuss the problem tomorrow at 10 A.M.
    C. Tomorrow morning at 10 A.M., the department manager will call you to discuss the problem.
    D. Tomorrow morning the department manager will call you to discuss the problem.

31. A conference on child care in the workplace the $200 cost of which to attend may be prohibitive to childcare workers who earn less than that weekly.
    A. A conference on child care in the workplace that costs $200 may be too expensive for childcare workers who earn less than that each week.
    B. A conference on child care in the workplace, the cost of which to attend is $200, may be prohibitive to childcare workers who earn less than that weekly.
    C. A conference on child care in the workplace who costs $200 may be too expensive for childcare workers who earn less than that a week.
    D. A conference on child care in the workplace which costs $200 may be too expensive to childcare workers who earn less than that on a weekly basis.

32. In accordance with estimates recently made, there are 40,000 to 50,000 nuclear weapons in our world today.
    A. Because of estimates recently, there are 40,000 to 50,000 nuclear weapons in the world today.
    B. In accordance with estimates made recently, there are 40,000 to 50,000 nuclear weapons in the world today.

C. According to estimates made recently, there are 40,000 to 50,000 weapons in the world today.
D. According to recent estimates, there are 40,000 to 50,000 nuclear weapons in the world today.

33. Motivation is important in problem solving, but they say that excessive motivation can inhibit the creative process. 33.____
    A. Motivation is important in problem solving, but, as they say, too much of it can inhibit the creative process.
    B. Motivation is important in problem solving and excessive motivation will inhibit the creative process.
    C. Motivation is important in problem solving, but excessive motivation can inhibit the creative process.
    D. Motivation is important in problem solving because excessive motivation can inhibit the creative process.

34. In selecting the best option calls for consulting with all the people that are involved in it. 34.____
    A. In selecting the best option consulting with all people concerned with it.
    B. Calling for the best option, we consulted all the affected people.
    C. We called all the people involved to select the best option.
    D. To be sure of selecting the best option, one should consult all the people involved.

35. There are a number of problems with the following letter. From the options below, select the version that is MOST in accordance with standard business style, tone, and form. 35.____

    Dear Sir:

    We are so sorry that we have had to backorder your order for 15,000 widgets and 2,300 whatzits for such a long time. We have been having incredibly bad luck lately. When your order first came in no one could get to it because my secretary was out with the flu and her replacement didn't know what she was doing, then there was the dock strike in Cucamonga which held things up for awhile, and then it just somehow got lost. We think it may have fallen behind the radiator.
    We are happy to say that all these problems have been taken care of, we are caught up on supplies, and we should have the stuff to you soon, in the near future—about two weeks. You may not believe us after everything you've been through with us, but it's true.
    We'll let you know as soon as we have a secure date for delivery. Thank you so much for continuing to do business with us after all the problems this probably has caused you.

    Yours very sincerely,
    Rob Barker

8 (#1)

A. Dear Sir:

   We are so sorry that we have had to backorder your order for 15,000 widgets and 2,300 whatzits. We have been having problems with staff lately and the dock strike hasn't helped anything.
   We are happy to say that all these problems have been taken care of. I've told my secretary to get right on it, and we should have the stuff to you soon. Thank you so much for continuing to do business with us after all the problems this must have caused you.
   We'll let you know as soon as we have a secure date for delivery.

   Sincerely,
   Rob Barker

B. Dear Sir:

   We regret that we haven't been able to fill your order for 15,000 widgets and 2,300 whatzits in a timely fashion.
   We'll let you know as soon as we have a secure date for delivery.

   Sincerely,
   Rob Barker

C. Dear Sir:

   We are so very sorry that we haven't been able to fill your order for 15,000 widgets and 2,300 whatzits. We have been having incredibly bad luck lately, but things are much better now.
   Thank you so much for bearing with us through all of this. We'll let you know as soon as we have a secure date for delivery.

   Sincerely,
   Rob Barker

D. Dear Sir:

   We are very sorry that we haven't been able to fill your order for 15,000 widgets and 2,300 whatzits. Due to unforeseen difficulties, we have had to back-order your request. At this time, supplies have caught up to demand, and we foresee a delivery date within the next two weeks.
   We'll let you know as soon as we have a secure date for delivery. Thank you for your patience.

   Sincerely,
   Rob Barker

KEY (CORRECT ANSWERS)

1.	D	11.	B	21.	C	31.	A
2.	A	12.	D	22.	B	32.	D
3.	B	13.	D	23.	D	33.	C
4.	A	14.	C	24.	C	34.	D
5.	B	15.	D	25.	B	35.	D
6.	C	16.	A	26.	D		
7.	B	17.	A	27.	A		
8.	D	18.	D	28.	B		
9.	A	19.	D	29.	C		
10.	C	20.	C	30.	B		

EXAMINATION SECTION
TEST 1

DIRECTIONS: In each of the following groups of four sentences, one sentence contains an error in sentence structure, grammar, usage, diction, or punctuation. Indicate the INCORRECT sentence.

1. A. To me this is truly a book that, after you have read it, you will find that it has unaccountably changed your way of viewing your surroundings.
    B. He had to learn the truth; therefore, he decided to visit the hospital.
    C. Turning the bend in the river, you face the rapids just ahead.
    D. We were terrified by sounds: the screaming of the wind; the restless rushing rustle of leaves in the trees; and the sudden, overwhelming, deafening explosions of thunder.

1.____

2. A. What can you do when he just shrugs his shoulders and says, "I give up"?
    B. His dog having barked a warning, the sentinel quickly adjusted his cap and peered out.
    C. The most radical innovation in the vehicle is the three wheels.
    D. Such people never have and never will be trusted.

2.____

3. A. Your employer would have been inclined to favor your request if you would have waited for an occasion when he was less busy.
    B. The fewer the chances for error, the less likely does error become.
    C. He has never stayed at the same hotel longer than two weeks.
    D. Though the world may blame us, neither he nor I am guilty of the crime.

3.____

4. A. We studied some mathematics, very well taught; some science and some French, both very badly taught; also some plays of Shakespeare, taught worse of all.
    B. They teased him mercilessly, but there was no doubt of him being able to take it and come back for more.
    C. In this country there are few chances of diversion—a shift in weather, perhaps, or something arriving in the mail.
    D. I find Henry James' prose style more difficult to read than James Joyce's.

4.____

5. A. Popular impressions about slang are often erroneous: there is no necessary connection, for example, between the slang and the vulgar, or between the slang and the ungrammatical; further, there is nothing new about the phenomenon of slang, nor is it anything peculiarly American.
    B. To know how to say what others only know how to think is what makes men poets or sages; and to dare to say what others only dare to think makes men martyrs or reformers or both.
    C. After all was said and done, after all the performers had finished their performances, I knew the winner to be he whom I singled out the moment I had met him.
    D. If once a man indulges himself in murder, very soon he comes to think little of robbery; and from robbing he next comes to drinking and Sabbath breaking, and from that to inactivity and procrastination.

5.____

6.
   A. What men, in their egoism, constantly mistake for a deficiency of intelligence in women is merely an incapacity for mastering that mass of male intellectual tricks, that complex of petty knowledges, that collection of cerebral rubber-stamps, which constitute the chief mental equipment of the average male.
   B. It is not easy to live in that continuous awareness of things which alone is true living.
   C. Every male peon had to go to a Pass Office and obtain a form, which he presents to his employer upon entering his employ, and who keeps it as long as the peon is with him.
   D. Other kinds of plants, as has been indicated previously, do better in marshy soils.

   6.____

7.
   A. Either the king or his advisers were mistaken.
   B. He was a man of talent too easily discouraged by criticism and who took too readily the advice of fools.
   C. Marx, indeed, supposed that once the revolution was successful in a great nation—he apparently thought it would come in the most advanced one of his day, Great Britain — it would spread at least to all the rest of the Western society, and therefore throughout the world.
   D. The evening was a huge success, for Cardin — and his gay, snappy clothes came out even better than in Paris.

   7.____

8.
   A. Smith asserted that whatever fame he enjoyed was due rather to chance than to talent.
   B. The prize will be awarded to whomever the committee agrees to give it to.
   C. Nor has the writer even the satisfaction of calling his reader a fool for misunderstanding him, since he seldom hears of it; it is the reader who calls the writer a fool for not being able to express himself.
   D. Struggling hard against almost insuperable odds, he was unable to effect even a small change in the course of the vehicle.

   8.____

9.
   A. The machine is not easy to fool, nor is it entirely foolproof.
   B. For all practical purposes history is, for us and for the time being, what we know it to be.
   C. In the free billowing fender, in the blinding chromium grille in the fluid control, in the ever-widening front seat, we see the flowering of the America that we know.
   D. He told an incredulous story of an encounter with a creature from outer space.

   9.____

10.
    A. He saw, facing him across the spring, a small man, his hands in his coat pockets, a cigarette slanted from his mouth.
    B. You must pay the fine unless you can prove that no traffic law was violated.
    C. I would rather have been a French peasant and worn wooden shoes.
    D. If we here in America cannot live peaceably and happily together, we cannot hope that nations that have different living conditions — different economic standards, different aspirations, different mores, different interests — to live peaceably with us.

    10.____

11.
    A. Neither Dr. Conant nor his followers knows what to do about the problem.
    B. Unbeaten thus far this year, the team won its seventh victory today.
    C. Must you lay the blame on the children?
    D. From the evidence, it is impossible to infer that he is guilty.

    11.____

12. A. The child whom I supposed to be the leader saw me, a misfortune that I had not anticipated.
     B. Although no dangerous chemicals had been left lying around, an explosion occurred; and the building with all the laboratories was destroyed.
     C. How can you function with the committee when you have no belief nor appreciation of the goals they have set up?
     D. Did you hear him say, "The end is near"?

13. A. The student demonstrations at Berkeley, to nobody's surprise, were not very different from any other large college.
     B. The heroine, whom everybody believed a well-known folk singer, bore the unlikely name of Letitia Delacroix.
     C. Paddling doggedly against the current, the river swirling about us, we managed at length to reach the shore.
     D. According to Miss Dew, the electronic clothes will be absolutely safe; the lamps give off no perceptible heat; and all the gadgetry snaps out.

14. A. Whether what they see is always worthwhile is of course debatable.
     B. Man has spun mythical genealogies and embroidered those that were actual.
     C. The doctor lost no time in telling him that he would have felt better if he would have taken his medicine on time.
     D. For all that he dislikes me, I still like him.

15. A. And so Pilate, willing to content the people, released Barabbas unto them.
     B. I shall welcome whomever wants to attend.
     C. Some such omissions are acceptable in speech but not in written English.
     D. The gentleman of our day is one who has money enough to do what every fool would do if he could afford it; that is, consume without producing.

16. A. The bureaucracy consists of functionaries; the aristocracy of idols; the democracy, of idolaters.
     B. Each person is born to one possession which overvalues all his others — his last breath.
     C. So I leave it with all of you: Which came out of the opened door — the lady or the tiger?
     D. Although I know this house and this neighborhood as well as I know myself, and although my friend here seems to know them hardly at all, nevertheless he has lived here longer than me.

17. A. In his effort to reach a wise decision about these truants, the attendance officer conferred many times with not only the parents and the principal, but also the dean and I.
     B. An old miser who picked up yellow pieces of gold had something of the simple ardor, something of the mystical materialism, of a child who picks out yellow flowers.
     C. There is no doubt that this particular fermentation of language has reached higher proportions in America than anywhere else.
     D. Dealers were instructed to replace all four steering arms bolted on the cars in question.

18. A. The manager told me he would have my car ready for me as soon as he can get the service department on the telephone.
    B. I come from a state that raises corn and cotton and cockleburs and democrats, and frothy eloquence neither convinces nor satisfies me.
    C. It recedes as fast on one side as it gains on the other.
    D. Certainly, whatever the source of his education, he acquired a sound knowledge of Latin, French, and Italian and a wide familiarity with the world of letters; and his career gave him an acquaintance with the world of people such as has fallen to the lot of few poets.

18._____

19. A. My greatest thirst is that which comes when I work hard in the strong sun.
    B. The doctor spoke but once; then I realized that it wasn't right for either her or me to ask that he repeat his message.
    C. As a vacation area, I think Florida is more preferable than California.
    D. By the time you arrive tomorrow, I shall have finished my work and yours.

19._____

20. A. Our main problem is the many pupils who come from broken homes.
    B. For years Joan has been attending summer camp and enjoying every minute of it.
    C. There is great narrative and dramatic power in Doctor Zhivago.
    D. Walt Whitman occupies a most unique place in literature.

20._____

21. A. The typist was pleased to note less mistakes on her paper this time; in fact, there were only three compared to ten on the earlier test.
    B. He said that if he had seen whoever it was who had erased the boards, he would have given that person a commendation card.
    C. Who did you say was responsible for this mess?
    D. Hold it as you would a pencil and press it firmly.

21._____

22. A. Give the book to whomever you see first when you enter the room.
    B. Some fans applaud rough basketball players; others, more sensitive, dislike these kind of athletes.
    C. The witness made a serious mistake when he took John's brother to be me.
    D. Not one of their friends approves of Robert's being the first of our graduates to enroll in a local college.

22._____

23. A. There are places outside the United States for which letter rates are the same as those charged for domestic mail.
    B. He does not doubt that he will succeed.
    C. The first couple to be married was Sarah and Jim.
    D. Bring this report on the students' failure to do their homework to the principal's office, which is two floors below this room.

23._____

24. A. He is seldom ever on time for this classes.
    B. Shall you return to New York City within a fortnight?
    C. Ever since, he has promised not to issue orders superseding those approved by the committee.
    D. She thought of how much more pleasant it would be to lie on the beach at Acapulco.

24._____

25. A. Think of the verb at first, not as one of the principal parts of speech, but as the hinge upon which many an effective sentence swings.
    B. Those who seek counsel from a book on writing are often disappointed.
    C. A large number of windows were broken by the mob.
    D. When I told him to stop working, he said he stopped a few minutes ago.

    25._____

26. A. He is one of those men who never care how they look.
    B. After the teacher had lain the book on the table, several pupils stopped to examine it.
    C. The acoustics in this room are not all they might be.
    D. Athletics have been virtually abolished from some smaller schools.

    26._____

27. A. Check all your data to see that they are an accurate reflection of the latest scholarship and research.
    B. One or the other of those books has presented a much better interpretation of the event than the text you are now studying.
    C. Neither the diplomats nor our president were to blame for the international fiasco.
    D. You or your friend seems to have broken the regulations.

    27._____

28. A. We shall report the accident to the policeman upon his arrival.
    B. Only one of the rooms which is vacant is on the fourth floor.
    C. Many up-to-date plans, some of which were immediately adopted, were submitted by the staff of architects.
    D. We find it to be a sheer waste of time to discuss matters in committee, the amount of the time required for establishing protocol being extremely excessive.

    28._____

29. A. Girls have little skill for, or interest in, auto mechanics.
    B. "Don Quixote," which is a fantasy to a child, is a work of sober philosophy to the serious thinker.
    C. Rather than ignore civil service, it would be advisable for you to consider its bearing on modern democracy.
    D. I don't doubt but what the party of my choice will win the election.

    29._____

30. A. We have done poorly, but the other party has done worse.
    B. The secret of happiness lies not in doing what you like, but to like what you do.
    C. It takes all kinds of readers to make a classic survive.
    D. In the van of the torchlight parade, carrying banners and slogans, marched my father and I.

    30._____

KEY (CORRECT ANSWERS)

1. A	11. A	21. A
2. D	12. C	22. B
3. A	13. A	23. D
4. B	14. C	24. A
5. C	15. B	25. D
6. C	16. D	26. B
7. B	17. A	27. C
8. B	18. A	28. B
9. D	19. C	29. D
10. D	20. D	30. B

TEST 2

DIRECTIONS: In each of the following groups, one of the four sentences contains an error in grammar, usage, diction, or punctuation. Indicate the INCORRECT sentence.

1. A. Do you think the situation is susceptible of improvement?
   B. He rejects the allegation since he feels he is completely innocent.
   C. This is the strangest sort of predicament I've ever been in.
   D. The largest amount of cars ever to cross the bridge in one day was reported for Sunday.

2. A. The Jones's house has been newly painted.
   B. He considered correct spelling his worst fault in English.
   C. "This machine," he declared, "will replace three or four men."
   D. The theatre is at Fourth Avenue and Sixty-eighth Street.

3. A. If he had kept his mind on his work, he would not now be in such straits.
   B. His graduation from High School was followed by a year of travel.
   C. Everyone rose to his feet as the visitor entered.
   D. About those things we talked later—years later.

4. A. The field that you have chosen is an interesting one, but offers less chances for advancement than the others.
   B. It appeared that he had lain there for many hours.
   C. The leader, with all his scores of followers, was arrested.
   D. There seems to be no alternative to violence.

5. A. If you are looking for a scapegoat, neither the boys down the street nor he was anywhere near the scene.
   B. How extremely difficult it is to decide whether or not to go to the performance!
   C. Of the two there is no question that this is the best choice.
   D. The auditorium in the Century Building was selected as the place for the meeting on the twenty-eighth.

6. A. Certainly there was no demand for, or need of, the gold-crusted dinnerware.
   B. This weather is much like April, except that it is much drier.
   C. Costume jewelry is not the sort of gift for her, you know.
   D. He could only smile at the absurdity of the request.

7. A. The injured player, his shoulder wrenched and his wind knocked out, was carried from the field and substitued by the second string quarterback.
   B. "It isn't everyone," he said, "who can act that well."
   C. The most expensive part of the entire trip was the hotel bills.
   D. The jury has announced its verdict.

8. A. A bright red hunting costume hung in the closet.
   B. I suggest that we give a prize to whoever gets three-quarters of the problems right.
   C. This is one of those essays that seek to preach a sermon.
   D. To play basketball well, passing must be practised.

69

9.
- A. The principal difficulty in examining these questions is that of determining the facts.
- B. He is, as I recall, taller than I.
- C. The main thing to see are the beautiful gardens.
- D. Three-fourths of the roof has been painted.

10.
- A. It's obvious that some of these are our's, some your's, and some their's.
- B. The dean wants us all—John, Helen, and me—to run for office.
- C. There are fewer reasons for supporting him than for opposing him.
- D. Amy's friends were interested in books and travel, as she was.

11.
- A. Rogers, who is responsible for all the action of the play, is an old man, very clever and witty.
- B. The 2's, 4's and 6's were in proper sequence.
- C. A teacher should not expect a pupil to know what he knows.
- D. I am in favor of his going, regardless of the consequences.

12.
- A. The leopard snarled viciously, sprang at the native who helpless screamed his fear.
- B. Do not feel bad about this unfortunate incident.
- C. From far above the clouds came the distant roar of the jets starting on their mission.
- D. Being now well advanced in years, he was proud of having served the people so well.

13.
- A. The reason so many came was that there had been a promise of refreshments.
- B. Regardless of what he says, I am going to choose my own friends.
- C. His job, it will be found, will be given to whomever has the ability to stand criticism.
- D. "You Are There" is the program I often listen to.

14.
- A. Rounding the curve and setting itself for the long pull over the mountain, the train began a labored puffing.
- B. Regardless of what he says, I am going to choose my own friends.
- C. His job, it will be found, will be given to whomever has the ability to stand criticism.
- D. He found the northern climate very healthful.

15.
- A. Yesterday marked the twelfth day I will have been attending the course.
- B. He had to walk a mile for some gasoline.
- C. Either the players or the umpire is to be interviewed.
- D. Don't begin your bickering just yet, please.

16.
- A. Although he is playing tennis only four years, we expect him to win the tournament.
- B. I have no alternative to following his request exactly as made.
- C. The group of "sidewalk superintendents" stood gaping in fascination at the demolition proceedings.
- D. Reviving momentarily, he tried to sit up, found the effort too much, sagged back, and lapsed into a coma.

17. A. Had the spectators remained calm, the poor, unfortunate children would not have been trampled.
    B. I have often heard her say, "Would that he had studied much harder!"
    C. Great writers, together with each background, is a fascinating study in itself.
    D. We cannot ever seem to find a person to whom responsibility is sacred.

17.____

18. A. There was always a disagreement as to who would do the work.
    B. I don't know that I can go.
    C. The lack of emphasis is caused by an involved sentence structure.
    D. No matter how gloomy the present news is, we should not break before it, but let us take courage.

18.____

19. A. The Egyptian delegate said that he might abstain from voting.
    B. We ought not to consider the lateness of the hour, not having made a real beginning on our task.
    C. If I started the task somewhat earlier, I would be finished now.
    D. The new regulations for handling a large fund are quite detailed and stringent.

19.____

20. A. These are the arguments against the plan: its uncertainty, its high cost, and its need for the kind of specialized personnel which is not available here.
    B. I don't think he would be interested in that kind of house.
    C. You're expected to take his lunch to him every day.
    D. Whomever he wished to destroy he first praised.

20.____

21. A. The lecture finished, the audience began asking questions.
    B. Any man who could accomplish that task the world would regard as a hero.
    C. Our respect and admiration are mutual.
    D. George did like his mother told him, despite the importunities of his playmates.

21.____

22. A. Pamphlets have circulated as widely as those published in this volume, and have been not less influential.
    B. He said he would go to the meeting provided that there were no change of plan.
    C. It is better to repose in the earth betimes than to sit up late; better than to cling pertinaciously to what we feel crumbling under us, and to protract an inevitable fall.
    D. As no one knows the truth as fully as him no one but him, can provide the testimony needed to clear the accused of very serious charges.

22.____

23. A. The Wesley brothers were dedicated reformers, and it is generally conceded that they helped to prevent a revolution in England.
    B. For the last three months, a boat had crossed daily from ship to shore and unloaded textiles, hardware, and tea — a magic ship, or so it seemed, for already ten times as much merchandise had been put ashore than there was room for in the hold.
    C. In her last letter she wrote, "Nothing else I have seen is so thrilling as Michelangelo's 'David.'"
    D. Schubert wrote "Die Forelle": Mme. Ostrawsky ruined it.

23.____

24.   A.   The artillery shell burst just as the men reached the shore with great violence.
      B.   The sergeant, an irritable fellow who was as strong as an ox and six feet tall, fixed an angry eye on the new recruit.
      C.   The question is not what we have done for the Allies, not what any other neutral country has done or has failed to do — such comparisons, I think, are far from the point.
      D.   One of the greatest barriers to clear understanding of objectives and methods by both officials and employees, and the public, is the growing tendency of administrative officials to clothe their thoughts and directives in a specialized language.

25.   A.   Then we had many resources; now, nothing.
      B.   As the gun opened fire (it was a .50-caliber gun), all movement ceased.
      C.   He said, "We shall adopt the slogan 'you can always take one with you'."
      D.   Requirements vary with the weather, in cold weather less water is needed for drinking and bathing.

26.   A.   The captain turned: "Who gave the order?"
      B.   Briefly, the functions of a military staff are to advise the commander, transmit his instructions, and the supervision of the execution of his decisions.
      C.   The art of war, like its weapons, is constantly developing, but 20th century technology has so speeded up the change that the military strategist now must run to keep pace.
      D.   The German theorist Clausewitz wrote texts that were studied by professional soldiers in every country that maintained a standing army.

27.   A.   The number of failures in the written test of the examination for the position as superintendent of the project were surprisingly low.
      B.   I appreciate your helping me do the dishes, but I wish you would lay them down on the table more carefully.
      C.   His understanding of the materials and processes involved in all of our operations is unrivalled in the industry.
      D.   No sooner had he begun to speak than an ominous muttering arose from the audience.

28.   A.   People who do not understand pigeons-and pigeons can be understood only when you understand that there is nothing to understand about them-should not go around describing pigeons or the effects of pigeons.
      B.   We see the moon by means of sunlight which falls upon it and is reflected back by its surface.
      C.   Looking through the main gate at the southwest corner of the park where the bridle path emerges from the wood, the blooming lilac can be seen in great sprays of purple, lavender, and white.
      D.   Although we both speak English, there seems to be a complete lack of communication between you and me.

29. A. He had better do as he is told unless he wants to get into trouble.
    B. Such a habit is not only dangerous to the individual's health but a man will find it a serious drain on his finances.
    C. After the mother had chid the child for spilling the milk, the father bade him leave the room.
    D. The saint is brushed in boldly in wide strokes, while the seraphim are traced in delicately in faint gray tones.

29._____

30. A. If he would have lain quietly as instructed, he might not have had a second heart attack.
    B. Shall you have cocktails served before dinner?
    C. John is likely to resent our refusal to accede to his demands.
    D. She saw that there was nothing else she could do; the room was as clean as it ever had been.

30._____

KEY (CORRECT ANSWERS)

1.	D	11.	C	21.	D
2.	B	12.	A	22.	D
3.	B	13.	B	23.	D
4.	A	14.	C	24.	A
5.	C	15.	A	25.	D
6.	B	16.	A	26.	B
7.	A	17.	C	27.	A
8.	D	18.	D	28.	C
9.	C	19.	C	29.	B
10.	A	20.	B	30.	A

TEST 3

DIRECTIONS: In each of the following groups of four sentences, one sentence contains an error in sentence structure, grammar, usage, diction, or punctuation. Indicate the INCORRECT sentence.

1. A. All this has made for confusion, for it needs heroic virtues to plunge into the muddy waters of the relevant literature to pluck out truth from their depths.
   B. In large organizations it is impossible for the head of the business to sign all the correspondence personally, although many of the letters may have to go out over his name, and he will accept responsibility for them.
   C. The list of essential occupations does not include workers engaged in the extermination of rodents and predatory animals except those in Government service.
   D. What a man cannot state, he does not perfectly know, and conversely, the inability to put his thoughts into words sets a boundary to his thought.

1.____

2. A. The foreign ministers of five Latin-American countries are the group now in conference.
   B. For breakfast the children ate prunes, cereal and milk, bacon, and hot chocolate.
   C. To gather data for this educational survey, teams of investigators have visited the elementary and junior high schools in New York City, including the private schools and the various parochial schools; the independent business schools specializing in shorthand, typing, and clerical skills; and the numerous trade schools.
   D. No matter what reasons or excuses are offered, there is only one word for his behavior: cowardice.

2.____

3. A. I do not think that this ought to mitigate against my chances of promotion.
   B. I have a surprise — but I won't tell you now.
   C. The Southern bloc talked for as long as they could.
   D. I've met two men who, I believe, were policemen.

3.____

4. A. There speaks one of those friends from whom the English language may well pray to be saved, one of the modern precisions who have more zeal than discretion.
   B. Whatever her thoughts, they were interrupted as the hotel lobby door opened and a young woman carrying a baby and her husband entered.
   C. Professional writers realize that they cannot hope to affect their readers precisely as they wish without care and practice in the proper use of words.
   D. Eminent men with a cure for the language, from Dean Swift to Lord Wavell, have from time to time proposed that an authority should be set up to preserve what is good and resist what is bad.

4.____

5. A. To avoid the hot sun, our plans were to travel at night.
   B. The use of radar, as well as the two-way radio, makes it possible for state troopers to intercept most speeders.
   C. The kindly nature-lover who first liberated a pair of gray squirrels has a great deal to answer for, including a large share of the salaries of numerous civil servants engaged on the task known to the, rather hopefully, as pest-elimination.
   D. The blame for this disorder rests not with Rome, nor with the bishops, nor with the parish priests, but with the ordinary man.

5.____

6. A. Each applicant was required to give his name, age, and where he lived.
    B. Andrew has been away for months; hence his bewilderment at these new laws is understandable.
    C. Whether he be vagabond or courtier, he may enter these portals.
    D. At the conference, it transpired that the president had absconded with the funds six months before.

7. A. Henry maintains that he has already read the article in its entirety.
    B. A large number of people signed the petition.
    C. We appreciate you going to all this trouble for us.
    D. The data which he collected are not relevant to this matter.

8. A. Do you believe that Ted is more brilliant than she?
    B. The lawn has been mowed, and the hedges trimmed.
    C. If one went into the hall, he told us, one could hear the wind screaming down the staircase.
    D. All the members of the club but him had come.

9. A. Alex is not so tall as his brother.
    B. The reason why I failed was that I had not studied my lesson.
    C. Their radio cost more than ours, but ours is equally good.
    D. The hostess only wanted the five couples to come for a week.

10. A. The pound sterling faces a critical test tomorrow when Britain's gold and foreign-exchange reserves position is expected to be disclosed.
    B. Under the support program farmers who cut back their acreage receive payment irrespective of when they sell the grain.
    C. "The call to war and boycott is increasingly discordant with the spirit and necessities of our times," the envoy said.
    D. The high cost and tightness of credit was the chief restraining factor in our economy last month.

11. A. "Neither I nor you," said Joe to his brother, "are able to fathom the rationale of women's styles."
    B. Many a man has wondered why, as the amount of cloth in ladies' dresses has diminished the price has increased.
    C. The flamboyant colors of shirtings have encouraged men to be bolder than they formerly were in the selection of sport clothes.
    D. In my opinion, however, nothing can be quite so colorful, I think, as the men's shorts displayed in the Greenwich Village shops.

12. A. Annoyed by her fall and uncertain of her status, the young lady left in a burst of tears and her limousine.
    B. Seeking a means of transportation, Bermuda's visitors have taken to bicycles, motor bikes, and scooters.
    C. I am determined that I will not pay tribute to anyone for any reason at any time.
    D. Issuing marriage licenses and performing marriages are only the beginning of the numerous duties of the City Clerk.

13.
 A. Oliver Wendell Holmes, Jr., decided to become a writer being that his father, the "autocrat of the breakfast table," was a successful author as well as a successful physician.
 B. Adult Westerns on TV have neglected the great tradition of bronco-busting in the Old West.
 C. Nothing would satisfy him but that I bow to his wishes.
 D. The two companies were hopeful of eventually effecting a merger, if the government didn't object.

13._____

14.
 A. The ore, pitchblende, is an important source of radium, which is found in many parts of the world.
 B. The ideal college for a student is one for which he is best fitted and in which he will be most at ease.
 C. Let's you and me settle the matter without consulting the committee.
 D. Nothing exasperates a grammarian more than to see an ungraceful expression become part of standard accepted speech.

14._____

15.
 A. The jury are still arguing over the credibility of one of the witnesses.
 B. If you would have considered all the alternatives logically, you would have chosen another course of action.
 C. He is different, in many respects, from his predecessor in the office of dean.
 D. Coming in on the bus, we can see the new atomic reactor plant.

15._____

16.
 A. Due to the mechanic's carelessness or a fault in the construction of the plane, forty lives were lost.
 B. Shelley and Dante were two famous poets who favored the terza rima; modern poets, on the other hand, find this pattern too restricting.
 C. The umpire said that the penalty would be meted out to whoever had been at fault.
 D. Look to mass media, for they may provide the next breakthrough in the training of science teachers.

16._____

17.
 A. You are sure to enjoy the performance, if only for the brilliant settings executed by a new designer.
 B. The language in Faulkner is somewhat like Proust, although Faulkner is much more inclined to sesquipedalianism.
 C. He said he thought he would buy two pairs of shoes and save one pair for special occasions.
 D. By tomorrow the book will have lain on the shelf, unread for two centuries.

17._____

18.
 A. The fact that Marie Curie's letters deal almost exclusively with science indicates that she must have had very few frivolous interests.
 B. Four former presidents of the United States have been graduated from Harvard University.
 C. The orchestra has risen as one man to applaud the conductor for his inspiring leadership of the symphony.
 D. Asia is as valuable and more fully developed than Africa.

18._____

19. A. Did you learn whether he was telling the truth?
     B. The story in the motion picture is different in only a few details from that in the story book.
     C. The invader effected an entry into the palace.
     D. My setter Pete can run as fast, if not faster than, your hound.

20. A. Each of us has chosen a book to read during the spring vacation.
     B. Neither Susanna nor her maids was aware of the watchers.
     C. Had I known his intentions, the outcome would have been different.
     D. After inhaling deeply he said, "This cigarette doesn't taste like tobacco."

21. A. The spectators thought the winner of the third race to be he.
     B. He it was who told the tale of hidden treasure.
     C. I inferred from his remarks that he had enjoyed himself.
     D. It was not his father's influence that led him to choose that kind of work.

22. A. He asked if they had read, "Ulysses."
     B. In her first attempt to make fudge, she concocted a nauseous mess that had to be thrown away.
     C. The insignia on his uniform indicate that he has served overseas.
     D. The program was broadcast by stations all over the world.

23. A. A visit to the children's ward of St. Giles' Hospital proved to be a heart-rendering experience.
     B. Let's you and me take the matter into our own hands.
     C. Being the only man in the group, he found that the demands upon his gentle-manliness exhausted him.
     D. The detective, when he was looking for a suspect, never dreamed of its being I.

24. A. Whom does he take me to be?
     B. His teachers realized that his absence was due to his illness.
     C. The Prospect Park carousel, which had been newly refurbished, became the center of attraction.
     D. There were less people than expected at the track meet last night.

25. A. Glancing rapidly over the report to stockholders which his secretary brought with the morning mail, the company's expenditures came to his attention.
     B. Of all natural beauties, none is fairer than these.
     C. They ate and drank and danced besides.
     D. These phenomena of spring never fail to reawaken man to joy and hope.

26. A. He had not only appeared in television, but in the movies as well.
     B. There are fewer chairs in the kitchen than in the parlor.
     C. Looking back, he could see his pursuers still swimming across the lake.
     D. A considerable portion of Rossetti's verse was written in his early life, but only a few of his poems were published then.

27.
   A. Existing statutes regarding monopoly practices are often so worded that it is difficult to determine precisely just what is a violation of the law.
   B. The reason the response to the speech was so weak was because it was over the heads of most of the audience.
   C. He, with his brothers and sisters, is about to leave for California.
   D. That kind of remark, you may be sure, will endear him to nobody.

27._____

28.
   A. Certain organ meats, like liver, we are told, are healthful.
   B. The shorter of the twins was also the prettier.
   C. The United States owns more gold bullion than any country in the world.
   D. When he returned, he discovered that his brother had been married.

28._____

29.
   A. Disenchantment with the domination of the living room by a big TV screen seems to be spreading among TV buyers.
   B. He asked to be let off at the intersection with the traffic light.
   C. I regard the inference of your remarks as highly insulting and altogether unwarranted.
   D. There is Dr. Johnson, a friend of my father's, whom I have not seen for many years.

29._____

30.
   A. I've known him for almost ten years, ever since the time that we worked together at a summer camp.
   B. No sooner had he entered the room when the lights went out.
   C. The plane having been grounded, he sent a telegram to his family telling them he would be late in returning.
   D. Of all flowers, roses, I think, smell sweeter.

30._____

31.
   A. John, who's mother is a teacher, is not as good a student as many other friends I have with no academic backgrounds in their families.
   B. On the other side of the coin, many of our major industrial concerns have been subjected to a constant stream of abuse.
   C. Vote for whoever, in your opinion, is most worthy of your consideration.
   D. He was graduated from college at the head of his class.

31._____

32.
   A. Each of the boys has to provide his own breakfast.
   B. Comparing his fortunes with other men's, he felt despondent.
   C. The difference between vegetable fats and animal fats is significant.
   D. Known to every man, woman, and child in the town, friends were never lacking to my grandfather.

32._____

33.
   A. After waiting in line for three hours, much to our disgust, the tickets had been sold out when we reached the window.
   B. That angry outburst of Father's last night resulted in our guests' packing up and leaving this morning.
   C. We have a new snobbery in the theatre, made up of that kind of people who will not sit beyond a certain row.
   D. The material contains wool and cotton fiber and is woven in a way different from any other I have seen.

33._____

34.
  A. When the members of the committee are at odds, when they are in the process of offering their resignations, problems become indissoluble.
  B. The interviewer should take extensive notes to serve as the basis of his rating and should identify and return these memoranda with his written report.
  C. Sharp advances last week in the wholesale price of beef chuck and moderate increases for fresh pork may be an indication of higher meat costs to come, but so far retail prices continue favorable.
  D. In fact, we must expect trouble throughout Africa, Latin America, and the Middle East as students from these regions are graduated from schools of subversion being operated in Moscow, Peking, and Havana.

35.
  A. "I don't like the present drift toward the welfare state, but I don't like implications that poverty is a 'political hallucination,'" wrote a woman who lives in the Middle West.
  B. Further acquaintance with the memoirs of Elizabeth Barrett Browning and Robert Browning enable us to appreciate the depth of influence that two people of talent can have on one another.
  C. The engagement party was hardly under way when the young man took his hat and his leave and was never heard of again.
  D. Would you explain to me how the new process differs from the old?

KEY (CORRECT ANSWERS)

1. B	11. D	21. A
2. C	12. A	22. A
3. A	13. A	23. A
4. B	14. A	24. D
5. A	15. B	25. A
6. A	16. A	26. A
7. C	17. B	27. B
8. B	18. D	28. C
9. D	19. D	29. C
10. D	20. B	30. B
	31. A	
	32. D	
	33. A	
	34. A	
	35. B	

TEST 4

DIRECTIONS: In each of the following groups of four sentences, one sentence contains an error in sentence structure, grammar, usage, diction, or punctuation. Indicate the INCORRECT sentence.

1.
   A. The printed material was prepared under adverse circumstances and distributed to all interested offices.
   B. Re-reading John Dos Passos U.S.A., one scene stuck in my mind.
   C. Separate vacations by husband and wife are much esteemed in certain circles, but if such holidays last more than a year or so, or if they involve close and prolonged contact with attractive members of the equal, opposite, and appreciated sex, even the most liberals raise their eyebrows.
   D. A sentence should give the impression of unit, of having a single forward thrust, of avoiding divergent ideas.

2.
   A. Jack said, "It was a good play;" but Bill disagreed with him.
   B. There are two objections to this plan: it is expensive and it is impractical.
   C. The conductor asked Jim and me to play a duet.
   D. His exposition is brilliant, his reports are as vivid as any novelists, and his understanding is very nearly without parallel.

3.
   A. He has an interest and an aptitude for his work
   B. Oh, that's what you said.
   C. Down from the hills came the outlaws to lay waste the countryside.
   D. We have rearranged the entire directory to make it easier to find people quickly.

4.
   A. He became a lawyer because it is interesting work.
   B. I shall send him rather than her.
   C. I set the can of paint on the window sill.
   D. I had just lain down when the telephone rang.

5.
   A. The regulations have not yet been published; nevertheless, we must proceed with the preparation of our course.
   B. Cases of this type either are far fewer in number or are not attended by the same administrative difficulties.
   C. His assignment was both to conduct the course and the evaluation of it.
   D. Unless compiled by June, the figures cannot be included in this year's annual report.

6.
   A. We had no sooner arrived than we were besieged by autograph fans.
   B. I enjoy football better than any sport.
   C. She felt very bad over his accident.
   D. Give the prize to whoever has won it.

7.
   A. The rocket soared gracefully aloft and then fell in the sea.
   B. Reaching the shelter, securing the shutters, starting a roaring fire, and shedding their frozen clothes all this was a matter of minutes.
   C. Without him, knowing the risks entailed in the venture, they forged ahead.
   D. The reason I enjoyed the performance was that it was well acted.

8. A. Come home with me for dinner, and I shall make steak and potatoes.
    B. Our youngest son was graduated from a military school last year.
    C. How does weather affect retail sales?
    D. We sell goods received from both government and non-government sources.

9. A. Considering the difficulties of the examination, I would say that our pupils gave a creditable performance.
    B. He gives generously to no less than six charitable organizations every month.
    C. A fine highway runs along beside the railroad tracks.
    D. He has a good chance to recover, provided he follows the doctor's advice.

10. A. He wastes more time than anyone else I know.
    B. He was the last murderer to be hanged in England.
    C. Since it rained continuously throughout the evening, the performance had to be canceled.
    D. A sound combination of work, play and rest has made him a healthy boy.

11. A. The chairman respectively submitted his report to the group.
    B. The more one eats, the more one wants.
    C. In my mind's eye, I can still see him laughing at problems that would crush another man.
    D. Neither the students nor the instructor is permitted to smoke in the classroom.

12. A. He had worked at the job only two months when he was obliged to leave in order to accompany his family to Nebraska.
    B. Losing his fortune in an investment in oil, he began life anew at fifty.
    C. There was the usual trio of three elderly, paunchy cigar-smoking men at the table in the corner.
    D. A first prize of some magnitude will be given to whoever can solve the puzzle.

13. A. It goes without saying that it is the teacher to whom the children look to for guidance, instruction, and assistance.
    B. He is one of the few candidates in this election who are deserving of our fullest confidence and respect.
    C. Tall, fair, active, educated, amiable, simple, carrying so naturally his great name, the happy youth, if he was one of the most ancient of princes, were one of the most modern of Romans.
    D. Common sense, as well as economics, tells us that what a country sells to other countries must be balanced by what it buys from abroad.

14. A. One of my favorite actors is Richard Burton, who you know often performs with his wife.
    B. Having been a teacher for years in schools from North Carolina to New York, these problems have been known to me for some time.
    C. If between you and me no compromise is possible, there seems little chance of our doing any business.
    D. I don't know who he could be.

15. A. The coach, with his entire team, was asked to the post-game reception. 15._____
    B. Unfortunately the child had drunk so much soda that he couldn't enjoy his meal.
    C. Neither the brothers nor their guardian are likely to get here before three o'clock.
    D. She and I are surely going to be invited to the party, but I for one have no intention of going.

16. A. "Whenever you come to see my new boat near Dock 17," said Mr. Jones, "Be sure to notice the name I chose for it." 16._____
    B. "Where," asked Bill plaintively, "is my new book?"
    C. "If you see Jack, please tell him to get back early," said Virginia. "I have some work for him to do."
    D. "No!" she cried, "We can't leave now."

17. A. Had he but known the doctor's name, much time would have been saved. 17._____
    B. If I were asked, or you were, I would not accept.
    C. He would reply if he could.
    D. Although he was an omnivorous reader, he will not read anything written by Jane Austen.

18. A. There are several aspects of Dickens' troubled life not yet fully explored. 18._____
    B. No one would want a doctor who has not proved his knowledge of biology and his ability to apply his knowledge to the State Medical Examiners.
    C. Many believe that the career of a lawyer is more interesting than that of a doctor.
    D. The popularity of Uncle Tom's Cabin effected many changes in public sentiment.

19. A. Interested in semaphore code, Betty joined the Girl Scouts to learn these kinds of signals. 19._____
    B. Harvard's football captain could tackle, block and pass better than anyone on the team.
    C. There is but one moving picture theater in all of New Cranford.
    D. Aunt Sally's strawberry shortcake certainly tasted good.

20. A. If I were you, I would enter the swimming meet. 20._____
    B. The accident would not have happened if Father had driven the car.
    C. You may sneer if you wish, but if it weren't for Westerns, there would be few television sponsors today.
    D. Byron always walks as if he was in a hurry.

21. A. Answer the door to whomever rings the bell. 21._____
    B. When the packages for us men arrived, there was a wild rush to open them.
    C. When a member of the group received a cake or a box of candy from home, he was expected to share it.
    D. Bill Simpson is one of the four men in our squad who have been on the honor list every term of his service.

22. A. Though Larry had awakened before the birds began to twitter, he lay in bed until long after the sun had risen. 22._____
    B. As Martha dived off the springboard, she was horrified to see that the water had been drained from the pool the night before.
    C. When he wrapped and addressed the package, he took it to the post office.
    D. There are still people who say that it has never really been proved that the earth is round.

23.
A. That house of my neighbor's is a disgrace to the entire block.
B. Mary was so disinterested in the baseball game that she yawned unashamedly.
C. John Kennedy effected many executive reforms during the tragically few years that he served as president.
D. If children are to remain healthy, they should be reared in a healthful environment.

24.
A. Today's Times has headlines about another girl who has just swum the English Channel.
B. If you ever visit Paris, you would sense for yourself the grace and charm of an old-world city that is forever new.
C. Placing his longbow on the grass beside him, Robin Hood, who had had an exciting day, lay down to rest and soon fell sound asleep; but so conditioned was he to impending danger that the softest footsteps would have awakened him instantly.
D. I was not at all surprised to hear of Jim Dolan's winning the poetry contest.

25.
A. Industry, as well as genius, was essential to the development of the automotive business.
B. Go at once if you can; if not, as soon as possible.
C. Why consult Harold, who knows nothing about the matter?
D. We the people of the United States, do ordain and establish this Constitution.

26.
A. We left the office together, he having finished his work.
B. We assumed the author of the letter to be he, as he had often made threats similar to those contained in it.
C. Whoever you say can do the job will be hired.
D. Everyone is expected to attend the afternoon session but the field supervisor, the custodian, and me.

27.
A. He cannot claim that his refusal to remit the proper sum was due to his not being informed of the requirement, for he was.
B. When you are entertaining a pot full of coffee is a good thing to have on hand.
C. Letters of censure and of commendation may be signed only by the Commissioner.
D. Although certain questions remain unanswered, the program is important and must go forward.

28.
A. His whereabouts has not yet been determined, though the police of several countries have been asked to look for him.
B. Anyone and everyone is invited to the annual charity ball given for the benefit of orphaned children.
C. If I were in your position and was offered a trip to Europe, I'd certainly go.
D. More than one vacation plan was changed because of the new requirement.

29. A. Battling the conservatives of his own party, the prime minister forced them to adopt his platform. 29.____
    B. The captain of the squad was a sophomore, one of last year's high school recruits, a player of great intelligence, and, above all, endurance.
    C. When equipped with overdrive transmission, an experienced driver can squeeze 18 to 20 miles a gallon out of a standard car.
    D. My memory of my aunt is very clear, yet my image of her is clouded by family tale and anecdote.

30. A. The lawyer who directed the investigation is the man whom we thought to be best qualified for the new post. 30.____
    B. Whether the report has been released or not will determine our action.
    C. The award will go to him who completes the course with the highest score.
    D. Proud of his skill in decanting, he poured some of the wine into his own glass first so that he would get the cork and not the lady.

31. A. The supervisor was advised to give the assignment to whoever, he believed, had a sense of responsibility. 31.____
    B. Hard-bitten, silent, resourceful, he was such a man as teen-age boys admire.
    C. Mary having been left behind to take care of the house, off the family went to Florida.
    D. After years of research, the United States Department of Health has issued a statement concerning the deleterious affects of cigarette smoking.

32. A. The founder and, for many years, the guiding spirit of "The Kenyon Review" is John Crowe Ransom, whom you must know as an outstanding American critic. 32.____
    B. When the reviews appeared in the morning papers, we saw that everybody but Carolyn and him had received adverse notices.
    C. Tyranny is one of those evils that tends to perpetuate itself.
    D. Little James' governess was a woman who should never have been allowed near a child.

33. A. Mr. Vondergrief, as a disinterested mediator, remained at the meeting all night in an effort to settle the strike. 33.____
    B. "For goodness' sake, children," cried the mother, "lower your voices!"
    C. An unpracticed liar, Mary explained her absence from school with an incredulous tale of derring-do in which she played the role of heroine.
    D. Regardless of what people say, I must repeat that these are the facts concerning the requirements for the position.

34. A. There is no objection to his joining the party if he is willing to fit in with the plans of the group. 34.____
    B. If you had seen the amount of pancakes he consumed at breakfast this morning, you might understand why he is so overweight.
    C. At five o'clock, this meeting will adjourn to the room next door.
    D. Ceremonies were opened by a drum and bugle corps of Chinese school children parading up Mott Street in colorful uniforms.

35. A. Neither the Bronte sisters nor their brother Branwell are remembered as healthy or happy.
    B. When my commanding officer first looked up from his desk, he took Lieutenant Baxter to be me.
    C. Having done exactly as he was told, the little boy came home expecting a reward in the form of a cookie or a piece of candy.
    D. Ever since his illness last winter, he has not looked well.

35.____

KEY (CORRECT ANSWERS)

1. B	11. A	21. A
2. D	12. C	22. C
3. A	13. A	23. B
4. A	14. B	24. B
5. C	15. C	25. D
6. B	16. A	26. B
7. A	17. D	27. B
8. A	18. B	28. C
9. B	19. B	29. C
10. A	20. D	30. D
	31. D	
	32. C	
	33. C	
	34. B	
	35. A	

EXAMINATION SECTION
TEST 1

DIRECTIONS: In each of the following groups, one of the four sentences contains an error in grammar, usage, diction, or punctuation. Indicate the INCORRECT sentence. *PRINT THE LETTER OF THE CORRECT ANSWER IN THE SPACE AT THE RIGHT.*

1. A. His vacuous expression suggested that he had been drugged.
    B. Poor business forced the company to plan drastic retrenchment.
    C. Everyone in town was trying to identify the anomalous donor.
    D. He blamed most of his failures on fortuitous circumstances.

    1.____

2. A. She divided the bread among them, without considering a share for herself.
    B. I should like to go, shouldn't you?
    C. All the boys did their work promptly so that they could leave early.
    D. Those kind of shoes are bad for the arches.

    2.____

3. A. Johnny ate the last three candies in the dish.
    B. He may sit between you and I for a while.
    C. Attempting to judge character by faces is an interesting pastime.
    D. They are not so willing to cooperate as they used to be.

    3.____

4. A. The two small chairs and the round table need to be reconditioned.
    B. Only the captain had been authorized to make such a decision.
    C. He asked the girl to bring the letter to her sister.
    D. No one seemed to know what his appointed task was.

    4.____

5. A. Data were collected, tabulated, filed and forgotten.
    B. Members of the scout troop immediately divided the chores between them.
    C. Reflecting on the incident, she acquired a new insight into his character.
    D. Because of the old man's temper everyone kept his opinion to himself.

    5.____

6. A. Bread and butter is a basic unit of the national diet.
    B. Beyond all doubt, it is we who must solve the problem.
    C. Looking into the matter, a startling situation came to light.
    D. Not everyone knows what his part in the undertaking is.

    6.____

7. A. No changes will be made, providing the money is returned immediately.
    B. To forget is understandable, but to ignore the call deliberately is unforgivable.
    C. He was named captain because of his strength.
    D. Please lay it on the table and leave it there.

    7.____

8. A. The rain having continued for a full hour without respite, the umpires called the game.
    B. Who do you think will win the next presidential election?
    C. The publisher offered no advance in royalties to the author nor a promise to advertise the book extensively.
    D. The tally showed seventeen ayes for the resolution.

    8.____

9. A. They thought they were cleverer than we.
    B. If the United States would not have acted promptly, South Korea would have been lost in two weeks.
    C. Everyone accepted the invitation except, oddly enough, him.
    D. All that was left was a few blackened tree stumps.

10. A. "Have you ever," Bill asked smugly, "tried to change a flat tire before?"
    B. Because of the damp weather the window wouldn't rise.
    C. The delegates chosen to represent our association are you, he, and I.
    D. To me, at least, the remark clearly inferred that she disbelieved the story.

11. A. We tiptoed quietly into the room and--over went the map with a crash!
    B. The manager, together with his two coaches, were engaging the umpire in a bitter controversy.
    C. There seem to be many sources of friction between the sergeant and his men.
    D. Every one of the contestants was jumpy and excitable before the race.

12. A. Maxwell spoke as though he meant every word he said.
    B. Richness of color and diversity of design distinguishes the new collection of imported fabrics.
    C. Give the prize to whoever deserves it.
    D. You will find ladies' and girls' clothing on the fourth floor.

13. A. Are the family in agreement on vacation plans?
    B. It is one of those planes that fly faster than the speed of sound.
    C. "We drove through sixteen states on our latest jaunt," she declared, "we had only one detour."
    D. There were but three of us left after the first ballots had been tabulated.

14. A. Mr. Smith demurred at first, but they insisted on his accompanying them.
    B. The data are embodied in the majority report.
    C. Perry never has and never will accept the point of view.
    D. The courier brought encouraging news: negotiations were still in progress.

15. A. Though we had ridden nearly six hundred miles in one day, we felt relatively fresh and rested.
    B. Neither the two oaks nor the maple was affected by the gales of near-hurricane force.
    C. So that Carl would be at his best for the examination, his mother insisted he go to bed early the night before.
    D. The audience showed its approval vigorously; they applauded, stamped their feet, and whistled.

16. A. Ted would have liked to have solved the problem.
    B. Had you completed the job by the time you left?
    C. "Who does he think he is?" she indignantly demanded.
    D. They told us that they had gone on a cruise for their vacation, but we have heard none of the details of their trip.

17. A. "I myself," declared his sprightly dinner partner, "was once a ballerina."   17.____
    B. It seems to be I who am most concerned about the defeat.
    C. Civilian defense is everybody's job, not just the worry of a few harried officials.
    D. The principal asked two of us, Carter and I, to assist in the gymnasium.

18. A. The general, after sifting all the evidence, decided that Lieutenant Jones, not his   18.____
       troops, was to blame.
    B. Paradoxical as it may seem, the millionaire's ambition is, not to make large sums
       of money, but rather for a name that future generations will remember.
    C. If we were to give up at this point, we should be guilty of treachery to posterity.
    D. All doctors agree that smoking and worry will aggravate any heart condition.

19. A. Now we can see that if we were more alert to the menace of Communism both   19.____
       here and abroad, we could have taken more vigorous steps to protect ourselves
       and our allies.
    B. "The time is now!" the Senator declared; "tomorrow may be too late."
    C. We wear machine-made clothes; we eat machine-made food; we sleep on
       machine-made beds.
    D. Did she say, "I shall never help that ingrate again"?

20. A. The criminal whom I believed to be him turned out to be a wholly different individ-   20.____
       ual.
    B. The woman was so sure of its being they that she flung the door open recklessly.
    C. What with her husband so much away, she is very lonesome.
    D. She had years of training with the best teachers in Europe, and now her voice is
       as sweet as a bird.

21. A. Of all the qualifications of a judge, the prime one is that he be disinterested.   21.____
    B. The author tries to say that women such as she are never able to make good in a
       competitive world.
    C. When Balboa and his men reached the summit, the Pacific could be seen glis-
       tening in the sunlight.
    D. Nobody but Margaret and her was able to come to the farewell party.

22. A. When Buckley arrived at the camp, he was told to report to his barracks, and that   22.____
       he would find his uniform there.
    B. Neither my friends nor I am to blame for the results of the last election.
    C. After you have read all the current books, you will agree with me that WINGS
       OVER ASIA is one of the best books that have been published this year.
    D. You will find that he is not the same man whom you met five years ago, so
       changed is he.

DIRECTIONS: In each of the following groups, one of the four sentences contains NO error in
             grammar, usage, diction, or punctuation. Indicate the CORRECT sentence.

23. A. A low ceiling is when the atmospheric conditions make flying inadvisable.   23.____
    B. They couldn't tell who the card was from.
    C. No one but you and I are to help him.
    D. To him fall the duties of foster parent.

24. A. They couldn't tell whom the cable was from.
    B. We like these better than those kind.
    C. It is a test of you more than I.
    D. The person in charge being him, there can be no change in policy.

25. A. Do as we do for the celebration.
    B. Do either of you care to join us?
    C. A child's food requirements differ from the adult.
    D. A large family including two uncles and four grandparents live at the hotel.

26. A. If they would have done that they might have succeeded.
    B. Neither the hot days or the humid nights annoy our Southern visitor.
    C. Some people do not gain favor because they are kind of tactless.
    D. No sooner had the turning point come than a new issue arose.

27. A. We haven't hardly enough time.
    B. He either will fail in his attempt or will seek other employment.
    C. After each side gave their version, the affair was over with.
    D. Every one of the cars were tagged by the police.

28. A. They can't seem to see it when I explain the theory.
    B. It is difficult to find the genuine signature between all those submitted.
    C. She can't understand why they don't remember who to give the letter to.
    D. Every man and woman in America is interested in his tax bill.

29. A. He arrived safe.
    B. I do not have any faith in John running for office.
    C. The musicians began to play tunefully and keeping the proper tempo indicated for the selection.
    D. Mary's maid of honor bought the kind of an outfit suitable for an afternoon wedding.

30. A. The new plant is to be electric lighted.
    B. The reason the speaker was offended was that the audience was inattentive.
    C. There appears to be conditions that govern his behavior.
    D. Either of the men are influential enough to control the situation.

31. A. If you would have listened more carefully, you would have heard your name called.
    B. Did you inquire if your brother were returning soon?
    C. We are likely to have rain before nightfall.
    D. Let's you and I plan next summer's vacation together.

32. A. There's a man and his wife waiting for the doctor since early this morning.
    B. The owner of the market with his assistants is applying the most modern principles of merchandise display.
    C. Every one of the players on both of the competing teams were awarded a gold watch.
    D. The records of the trial indicated that, even before attaining manhood, the murderer's parents were both dead.

33. A. Why don't you start the play like I told you?
    B. I didn't find the construction of the second house much different from that of the first one I saw.
    C. "When", inquired the child, "Will we begin celebrating my birthday?"
    D. There isn't nothing left to do but not to see him anymore.

34. A. The child could find neither the shoe or the stocking.
    B. The musicians began to play tunefully and keeping the proper tempo indicated for the selection.
    C. The amount of curious people who turned out for Opening Night was beyond calculation.
    D. "Indeed," mused the poll-taker, "The winning candidate is much happier than I."

35. A. Just as you said, I find myself gaining weight.
    B. A teacher should leave the capable pupils engage in creative activities.
    C. The teacher spoke continually during the entire lesson, which, of course, was poor procedure.
    D. Mary's maid of honor bought the kind of an outfit suitable for an afternoon wedding.

36. A. The new schedule of working hours and rates was satisfactory to both employees and employer.
    B. Many common people feel keenly about the injustices of Power Politics.
    C. Mr. and Mrs. Burns felt that their grandchild was awfully cute when he waved good-bye.
    D. The tallest of the twins was also the most intelligent.

37. A. Do you intend bringing most of the refreshments yourself?
    B. Suffering from a severe headache all day one dose of the prescribed medicine relieved me.
    C. "Please let my brothers and I help you with your packages," said Frank to Mrs. Powers.
    D. Every one of the rooms we visited had displays of pupils' work in them.

38. A. The telephone linesmen, working steadily at their task during the severe storm, the telephones soon began to ring again.
    B. Meat, as well a fruits and vegetables, is considered essential to a proper diet.
    C. He looked like a real good boxer that night in the ring.
    D. The man has worked steadily for fifteen years before he decided to open his own business.

39. A. No one can foretell when I will have another opportunity like that one again.
    B. The last group of paintings shown appear really to have captured the most modern techniques.
    C. We searched high and low, both in the attic and cellar, but were unsuccessful in locating mementos.
    D. None of the guests was able to give the rules of the game accurately.

40. A. After the debate, every one of the speakers realized that, given another chance, he could have done better.
    B. The reason given by the physician for the patient's trouble was because of his poor eating habits.
    C. The fog was so thick that the driver couldn't hardly see more than ten feet ahead.
    D. I suggest that you present the medal to who you think best.

41. A. A decision made by a man without much deliberation is sometimes no different than a slow one.
    B. By the time Mr. Brown's son will graduate Dental School, he will be twenty-six years of age.
    C. Who did you predict would win the election?
    D. The auctioneer had less stamps to sell this year than last year.

42. A. Having pranced into the arena with little grace and unsteady hoof for the humps ahead, the driver reined his horse.
    B. Once the dog wagged it's tail, you knew it was a friendly animal.
    C. The record of the winning team was among the most note-worthy of the season.
    D. When asked to choose corn, cabbage, or potatoes, the diner selected the latter.

43. A. The maid wasn't so small that she couldn't reach the top window for cleaning.
    B. Many people feel that powdered coffee produces a really good flavor.
    C. Would you mind me trying that coat on for size?
    D. This chair looks much different than the chair we selected in the store.

44. A. After trying unsuccessfully to land a job in the city, Will located in the country on a farm.
    B. On the last attempt, the pole-vaulter came nearly to getting hurt.
    C. The observance of Armistice Day throughout the world offers an opportunity to reflect on the horrors of war.
    D. Outside of the mistakes in spelling, the child's letter was a very good one.

45. A. Scissors is always dangerous for a child to handle.
    B. I assure you that I will not yield to pressure to sell my interest.
    C. Ask him if he has recall of the incident which took place at our first meeting.
    D. The manager felt like as not to order his usher-captain to surrender his uniform.

46. A. The mother of the bride climaxed the occasion by exclaiming, "I want my children should be happy forever."
    B. We read in the papers where the prospects for peace are improving.
    C. "Can I share the cab with you?" was frequently heard during the period of gas rationing.
    D. Had the police suspected the ruse, they would have taken proper precautions.

47. A. The teacher admonished the other students neither to speak to John, nor should they annoy him.
    B. Fortunately we had been told that there was but one service station in that area.
    C. An usher seldom rises above a theatre manager.
    D. The epic, GONE WITH THE WIND, is supposed to have taken place during the Civil War Era.

48. A. Shall you be at home, let us say, on Sunday at two o'clock?
     B. We see Mr. Lewis take his car out of the garage daily, newly polished always.
     C. We have no place to keep our rubbers, only in the hall closet.
     D. Isn't it true what you told me about the best way to prepare for an examination?

49. A. The host thought the guests were of the hungry kinds so he prepared much food.
     B. The museum is often visited by students who are fond of early inventions, and especially patent attorneys.
     C. I rose to nominate the man who most of us felt was the most diligent worker in the group.
     D. The child was sent to the store to purchase a bottle of milk, and brought home fresh rolls, too.

50. A. The garden tool was sent to be sharpened, and a new handle to be put on.
     B. At the end of her vacation, Joan came home with little money, but which systematic thrift soon overcame.
     C. We people have opportunities to show the rest of the world how real democracy functions.
     D. The guide paddled along, then fell in a reverie which he related the history of the region.

KEY (CORRECT ANSWERS)

1. C	11. B	21. C	31. C	41. C
2. D	12. B	22. A	32. B	42. C
3. B	13. C	23. D	33. B	43. B
4. C	14. C	24. A	34. D	44. C
5. B	15. D	25. A	35. A	45. B
6. C	16. A	26. D	36. A	46. D
7. A	17. D	27. B	37. A	47. B
8. C	18. B	28. D	38. B	48. A
9. B	19. A	29. A	39. D	49. C
10. D	20. D	30. B	40. A	50. C

TEST 2

DIRECTIONS: In each of the following groups, one of the four sentences contains NO error in grammar, usage, diction, or punctuation. Indicate the CORRECT sentence. *PRINT THE LETTER OF THE CORRECT ANSWER IN THE SPACE AT THE RIGHT.*

1.
   A. We should have investigated the cause of the noise by bringing the car to a halt.
   B. The first few strokes of the brush were enough to convince me that Tom could paint much better than me.
   C. We inquired if we could see the owner of the store, after we waited for one hour.
   D. The highly-strung parent was aggravated by the slightest noise that the baby made.

   1.___

2.
   A. The police, investigating the crime, were successful in discovering only one possibly valuable clue.
   B. Due to an unexpected change in plans, the violin soloist did not perform.
   C. Besides being awarded a Bachelor's degree at college, the scientist has since received many honorary degrees.
   D. The data offered in advance of the recent Presidential election seems to have possessed elements of inaccuracy.

   2.___

3.
   A. I don't quite see that I will be able to completely finish the job in time.
   B. By my statement, I infer that you are guilty of the offense as charged.
   C. Wasn't it strange that they wouldn't let no one see the body?
   D. I hope that this is the kind of rolls you requested me to buy.

   3.___

4.
   A. He said he preferred the climate of Florida to California.
   B. Because of the excessive heat, a great amount of fruit juice was drunk by the guests.
   C. This week's dramatic presentation was neither as lively nor as entertaining as last week.
   D. The fashion expert believed that no one could develop new creations more successfully than him.

   4.___

5.
   A. That kind of orange is grown only in Florida.
   B. Walking up the rickety stairs, the bottle slipped from his hands and smashed.
   C. The reason they granted his request was because he had a good record.
   D. Little Tommy was proud that the teacher always asked him to bring messages to the office.

   5.___

6.
   A. The new mayor is a resident of this city for thirty years.
   B. Do you mean to imply that had he not missed that shot he would have won?
   C. Next term I shall be studying French and history.
   D. I read in last night's paper where the sales tax is going to be abolished.

   6.___

7.
   A. To have children vie against one another is psychologically unsound.
   B. Would anyone else care to discuss his baby?
   C. He was interested and aware of the problem.
   D. I sure would like to discover if he is motivating the lesson properly.

   7.___

8. A. She graduated Barnard College twenty-five years ago.
    B. He studied the violin since he was seven.
    C. She is not so diligent a researcher as her classmate.
    D. He discovered that the new data corresponds with the facts disclosed by Werner.

9. A. You have three alternatives: law, dentistry, or teaching.
    B. If I would have worked harder, I would have accomplished my purpose.
    C. He affected a rapid change of pace and his opponents were outdistanced.
    D. He looked prosperous, although he had been unemployed for a year.

10. A. Tell me where you hid it, no one shall ever find it.
    B. They lay in the sun for many hours, getting tanned.
    C. The reproduction arrived, and had been hung in the living room.
    D. First begin by calling the roll.

11. A. Deliver these things to whomever arrives first.
    B. Everybody but she and me is going to the conference.
    C. If the number of patrons is small, we can serve them.
    D. When each of the contestants find their book, the debate may begin.

12. A. After his illness, he stood in the country three weeks.
    B. If you wish to effect a change, submit your suggestions.
    C. It is silly to leave children play with knives.
    D. Play a trick on her by spilling water down her neck.

DIRECTIONS: In each of the following groups, one of the four sentences contains an error in grammar, usage, diction, or punctuation. Indicate the INCORRECT sentence.

13. A. Do you think the situation is susceptible of improvement?
    B. He rejects the allegation, since he feels he is completely innocent.
    C. This is the strangest sort of predicament I've ever been in.
    D. The largest amount of cars ever to cross the bridge in one day was reported for Sunday.

14. A. The Jones's house has been newly painted.
    B. He considered correct spelling his worst fault in English.
    C. "This machine," he declared, "will replace three or four men."
    D. The theatre is at Fourth Avenue and Sixty-eighth Street.

15. A. If he had kept his mind on his work, he would not now be in such straits.
    B. His graduation from High School was followed by a year of travel.
    C. Everyone rose to his feet as the visitor entered.
    D. About those things we talked later—years later.

16. A. The field that you have chosen is an interesting one, but offers less chance for advancement than the others.
    B. It appeared that he had lain there for many hours.
    C. The leader, with all his scores of followers, was arrested.
    D. There seems to be no alternative to violence.

17.
   A. If you are looking for a scapegoat, neither the boys down the street nor he was anywhere near the scene.
   B. How extremely difficult it is to decide whether or not to go to the performance!
   C. Of the two there is no question that this is the best choice.
   D. The auditorium in the Century Building was selected as the place for the meeting on the twenty-eighth.

17.___

18.
   A. Certainly there was no demand for, or need of, the gold-encrusted dinnerware.
   B. This weather is much like April, except that it is much drier.
   C. Costume jewelry is not the sort of gift for her, you know.
   D. He could only smile at the absurdity of the request.

18.___

19.
   A. The injured player, his shoulder wrenched and his wind knocked out, was carried from the field and substituted by the second string quarterback.
   B. "It isn't everyone," he said, "who can act that well."
   C. The most expensive part of the entire trip was the hotel bills.
   D. The jury has announced its verdict.

19.___

20.
   A. A bright red hunting costume hung in the closet.
   B. I suggest that we give a prize to whoever gets three-quarters of the problems right.
   C. This is one of those essays that seek to preach a sermon.
   D. To play basketball well, passing must be practiced.

20.___

21.
   A. The principal difficulty in examining these questions is that of determining the facts.
   B. He is, as I recall, taller than I.
   C. The main thing to see are the beautiful gardens.
   D. Three-fourths of the roof has been painted.

21.___

22.
   A. It's obvious that some of these are our's, some your's, and some their's.
   B. The dean wants us all—John, Helen, and me—run for office.
   C. There are fewer reasons for supporting him than for opposing him.
   D. Amy's friends were interested in books and travel, as she was.

22.___

23.
   A. Rogers, who is responsible for all the action of the play, is an old man, very clever and witty.
   B. The 2's, 4's and 6's were in proper sequence.
   C. A teacher should not expect a pupil to know what he knows.
   D. I am in favor of his going, regardless of the consequences.

23.___

24.
   A. The leopard snarled viciously, sprang at the native who helpless screamed his fear.
   B. Do not feel bad about this unfortunate incident.
   C. From far above the clouds came a distant roar of the jets starting on their mission.
   D. Being now well advanced in years, he was proud of having served the people so well.

24.___

25.
   A. The reason so many came was that there had been a promise of refreshments.
   B. No sooner had the guest speaker arrived when it began to rain.
   C. They do not always hire whoever has the most experience.
   D. He found the northern climate very healthful.

25.___

26.
  A. Rounding the curve and setting itself for the long pull over the mountain, the train began a labored puffing.
  B. Regardless of what he says, I am going to choose my own friends.
  C. The job, it will be found, will be given to whomever has the ability to stand criticism.
  D. "You Are There" is the program I often listen to.

27.
  A. Yesterday marked the twelfth day I will have been attending the course.
  B. He had to walk a mile for some gasoline.
  C. Either the players or the umpire is to be interviewed.
  D. Don't begin your bickering just yet, please.

28.
  A. Although he is playing tennis only four years, we expect him to win the tournament.
  B. I have no alternative to following his request exactly as made.
  C. The group of "sidewalk superintendents" stood gaping in fascination at the demolition proceedings.
  D. Reviving momentarily, he tried to sit up, found the effort too much, sagged back, and lapsed into a coma.

29.
  A. Had the spectators remained calm, the poor, unfortunate children would not have been trampled.
  B. I have often heard her say, "Would that he had studied much harder!"
  C. Great writers, together with each background, is a fascinating study in itself.
  D. We cannot ever seem to find a person to whom responsibility is sacred.

30.
  A. There was always a disagreement as to who would do the work.
  B. I don't know that I can go.
  C. The lack of emphasis is caused by an involved sentence structure.
  D. No matter how gloomy the present news is, we should not break before it, but let us take courage.

31.
  A. The Egyptian delegate said that he might abstain from voting.
  B. We ought not to consider the lateness of the hour, not having made a real beginning on our task.
  C. If I started the task somewhat earlier, I would be finished now.
  D. The new regulations for handling a large fund are quite detailed and stringent.

32.
  A. These are the arguments against the plan: its uncertainty, its high cost, and its need for the kind of specialized personnel which is not available here.
  B. I don't think he would be interested in that kind of house.
  C. You're expected to take his lunch to him every day.
  D. Whomever he wished to destroy he first praised.

33.
  A. The lecture finished, the audience began asking questions.
  B. Any man who could accomplish that task the world would regards as a hero.
  C. Our respect and admiration are mutual.
  D. George did like his mother told him, despite the importunities of his playmates.

34.
- A. Each applicant was required to give his name, age, and where he lived.
- B. Andrew has been away for months; hence his bewilderment at these new laws is understandable.
- C. Whether he be vagabond or courtier, he may enter these portals.
- D. At the conference, it transpired that the president had absconded with the funds six months before.

35.
- A. Henry maintains that he has already read the article in its entirety.
- B. A large number of people signed the petition.
- C. We appreciate you going to all this trouble for us.
- D. The data which he collected are not relevant to the matter.

36.
- A. Do you believe that Ted is more brilliant than she?
- B. There isn't but one grocery store in the neighborhood.
- C. If one went into the hall, he told us, one could hear the wind screaming down the staircase.
- D. All the members of the club but him had come.

37.
- A. Alex is not so tall as his brother.
- B. The reason why I failed was that I had not studied my lesson.
- C. Their radio cost more than ours, but ours is equally good.
- D. The hostess only wanted the five couples to come for a week.

38.
- A. A good prayer for this season is that the mutual distrust of Russia and the free countries of the world will not lead to war.
- B. The fellow who, in our ignorance, we were inclined to censure proved to be quite admirable.
- C. The euphemistic use of some words is to be deprecated, because it tends to drive them out of currency.
- D. I was so nauseated by the stench from the marshes that I could not enjoy the trip.

39.
- A. Providing us with a long list of names of possible successors, he proffered his resignation.
- B. The data on this as well as on the other proposal is clearly set forth in the report.
- C. It was agreed that his salary would be increased by fifty percent, provided he could settle his affairs here and sail on the first of April.
- D. Nothing was further from my mind than the thought that you had misrepresented your connection with the firm.

40.
- A. It is most likely that he has decided to postpone making a report until he has consulted his lawyer.
- B. Now I shall answer his most recent inquiry: "When are we going to receive the shipment of goods"?
- C. Possibly, though not probably, we shall be able to adapt the old machines to our present needs; such an arrangement, however, if it is made, should surely be a temporary one.
- D. The article defended, although not definitely stating them, many theories to which I cannot subscribe.

41.
- A. We could see no way out of the impasse except for them to make an apology.
- B. The program would have been a great disappointment had it not been for the second number's charm and finesse.
- C. That a prisoner chafes at his captivity is not at all surprising to a person who is realistic.
- D. We thought her to be the one whom the great majority of the group would decide should be chosen as the winner.

41.____

42.
- A. There can be little doubt that this fabric is as durable or even more durable than the other.
- B. We had but to say the word and we could have had our every wish fulfilled.
- C. I am not used to this type of report; please revise it, deleting the details.
- D. The day, which had dawned cloudy and dull, cleared perceptibly as we started on our journey.

42.____

43.
- A. By the time you read this letter, I shall have been in England more than a week.
- B. See pp. 53-55 for an explanation of the rules governing the use of the apostrophe.
- C. All his 5's looked like 3's; it was well nigh impossible to add correctly a column of figures which he had copied.
- D. If they would have known the probable outcome, they would never have cast their votes for that candidate.

43.____

44.
- A. In the doctor's opinion, a cure will not be affected by the present treatment.
- B. Neither you, who are her closest friends, nor my sister are to blame in this matter.
- C. The crowd tossed their hats into the air when the home team scored a touchdown.
- D. This pair of scissors is too dull to cut so thick a cloth as denim.

44.____

45.
- A. They were so timid, so fearful, and so nervous that I objected to him mentioning the accident in his oral report to them.
- B. A colon, or colon and dash, may precede an enumeration, a long direct quotation, or a statement formally introduced, especially with "as follows," "namely," etc.
- C. "Who's doubting your word? You're too sensitive," he said, as he hurriedly left the room.
- D. Nobody but him and his classmates was able to see the difference between the twins.

45.____

46.
- A. Their enthusiasm entirely spent, they were reluctant to enter another contest.
- B. A walking tour through that state is not to be contemplated because every resident is liable to demand several kinds of identification.
- C. We want only such preparation as will make success certain.
- D. If you would make sure that the plan is feasible, show it to the floor manager.

46.____

47.
- A. "We'd have liked to go along," I said, "if you'd only thought to invite us."
- B. They thought it to be him.
- C. Do you mean to infer in those slighting remarks that I have neglected my duty?
- D. At last, we were gathered all together again, like birds in a nest.

47.____

48.   A. He asked his daughter whether she would be willing to devote her spare time to the planning of a series of programs for children.
      B. It is not the purpose of the proposed legislation that all men should be cared for from the cradle to the grave, but to prevent any recurrence of widespread poverty among our citizens.
      C. If there is clearly no solution to their problem, let's turn our attention at once to the next item.
      D. His voice sounded like a frog's, although he had had several years' training in both music and speech

49.   A. He should be allowed to make the experiment without let or hindrance.
      B. In spite of their docility, the children presented some real problems to the teachers when they first met them after their vacation.
      C. Neither he nor I am concerned about the matter.
      D. Since we have the "know-how," it is our duty to undertake the assignment.

50.   A. Let us—you, who are a foreigner, and I, who am a native,—try to see the problems without bias.
      B. All things considered, we can reach no other decision.
      C. We originally considered him to be the person most likely to win.
      D. Men's, women's, boys' and girls' interests vary so much that it is difficult to plan an effective program for the meeting.

KEY (CORRECT ANSWERS)

1. A	11. C	21. C	31. C	41. D
2. B	12. B	22. A	32. B	42. A
3. D	13. D	23. C	33. D	43. D
4. B	14. B	24. A	34. A	44. B
5. A	15. B	25. B	35. C	45. A
6. B	16. A	26. C	36. B	46. B
7. B	17. C	27. A	37. D	47. C
8. C	18. B	28. A	38. B	48. B
9. D	19. A	29. C	39. B	49. B
10. A	20. D	30. D	40. B	50. A

EXAMINATION SECTION
TEST 1

DIRECTIONS: In each of the following groups, one of the four sentences contains an error in grammar, usage, diction, or punctuation. Indicate the INCORRECT sentence. *PRINT THE LETTER OF THE CORRECT ANSWER IN THE SPACE AT THE RIGHT.*

1.
   A. If I were you, he should not be allowed to regret having befriended the child.
   B. Deserted, surrounded and outnumbered, and with everything at stake, their refusal to surrender took great courage.
   C. Considering all his efforts in our behalf, our warmest thanks were clearly merited by him.
   D. He enjoyed, in his mountain retreat, not only skimming over the ice on his skates, but also feeling the danger of a mad rush down perilous slopes on his bobsled.

   1._____

2.
   A. A young author is apt to run into a confusion of mixed metaphors which leaves the sense disjointed and the imagination distracted.
   B. We do not intend, in enforcing this rule, to guarantee your safety under all conditions; however, under ordinary circumstances, you will find you are adequately protected.
   C. When John entered the room, he shouted, "Run for your lives!" and then sat down quietly at the piano.
   D. My friend Eldridge has bought a plot of ground and intends to build a small house upon it within the year.

   2._____

3.
   A. The students in the dormitories were forbidden, unless they had special passes, from staying out after 11:00 P.M.
   B. The Student Court rendered a decision satisfactory to both the defendant and the accuser.
   C. Margarine is being substituted for butter to a considerable extent.
   D. In this school there are at least fifteen minor accidents a year which are due to this traffic violation.

   3._____

4.
   A. Everyone at camp must have his medical certificate on file before participating in competitive sports.
   B. A crate of oranges were sent from Florida for all the children in Cabin Six.
   C. John and Danny's room looks as if they were prepared for inspection.
   D. Three miles is too far for a young child to walk.

   4._____

5.
   A. Sailing along New England's craggy coastline, you will relive a bygone era of far-roving whalers and graceful clipper ships.
   B. The march of history is reenacted in folk festivals, outdoor pageants, and fiestas local in theme, but national in import.
   C. Visiting the scenes of the past, our interest in American history is renewed and enlivened.
   D. What remained was a few unrecognizable fragments.

   5._____

6. A. The game over, the spectators rushed out on the field and tore down the goalposts.
    B. The situation was aggravated by disputes over the captaincy of the team.
    C. Yesterday they lay their uniforms aside with the usual end-of-the season regret.
    D. It is sometimes thought that politics is not for the high-minded.

7. A. Sandburg's autobiography, as well as his poems, are familiar to many readers.
    B. A series of authentic records of the American Indian tribes is being published.
    C. The Smokies are the home of the descendants of this brave tribe.
    D. Five dollars is really not too much to pay for a book of this type.

8. A. No one but her could have recognized him.
    B. She knew the stranger to be him whom she had given up as lost.
    C. He looked like he had been in some strange land where age advanced at a double pace.
    D. It is impossible to include that item; the agenda have already been mimeographed.

9. A. You have probably heard of the new innovation in the regular morning broadcast.
    B. During the broadcast you are expected to stand, to salute, and to sing the fourth stanza of "America."
    C. None of the rocks which form the solid crust of our planet is more than two billions years old.
    D. "I have finished my assignment," said the pupil. "May I go home now?"

10. A. The text makes the process of developing and sustaining a successful home zoo appear to be a pleasant profitable one.
    B. The warmth and humor, the clear characterization of the Walmsey family, which includes three children, two dogs, and two cats, is such fun to read that this reviewer found herself reading it all over again.
    C. You will be glad, I am sure, to give the book to whoever among your young friends has displayed an interest in animals.
    D. The consensus among critics of children's literature is that the book is well worth the purchase price.

11. A. Participation in active sports produces both release from tension as well as physical well-being.
    B. The problem of taxes is still with them.
    C. Every boy and every girl in the auditorium was thrilled when the color guard appeared.
    D. At length our club decided to send two representatives to the meeting, you and me.

12. A. B. Nelson & Co. has a sale of dacron shirts today.
    B. Venetian blinds-called that although they probably did not originate in Venice-are no longer used as extensively as they were at one time.
    C. He determined to be guided by the opinion of whoever spoke first.
    D. There is often disagreement as to whom is the better Shakespearean action, Evans or Gielgud.

13. A. Remains of an ancient civilization were found near Mexico City.
    B. It is interesting to compare the interior of one of the pyramids in Mexico to the interior of one of the pyramids in Egypt.
    C. In two days' journey you will be reminded of political upheavals comparable to the volcanic eruptions still visible and audible in parts of Mexico.
    D. There is little danger of the law's being broken, so drastic is the penalty.

    13._____

14. A. It did not take him long to develop an interest in the great American pastime - baseball.
    B. If you had made your way to the Whipsnade Zoo, you would have had an opportunity of seeing wild animals in more or less natural habitats.
    C. How I should have liked to have spent a few more days in Paris!
    D. Neither baseball pools nor any other form of gambling is allowed in or near the school.

    14._____

15. A. If the bill were introduced, it would provoke endless debate.
    B. Since George, with his two dogs, is to be with us, it might be better to rent a cabin.
    C. He, not I, is the one to decide.
    D. He is, however, one of those restless people who never seems content in his present environment.

    15._____

16. A. Instead of looking disdainfully at London grime, think of it as a mantle of tradition.
    B. Nobody but the pilot and the co-pilot was permitted to handle the mysterious package.
    C. Not only is industry anxious to hire all available engineers, but they are being offered commissions by the armed forces.
    D. For immediate service go direct to the store manager.

    16._____

17. A. The delegates alighted and started off in a taxi, their baggage having been taken care of.
    B. That kind of potatoes is grown in Idaho.
    C. Besides Alan Stevens, there were eight officers of the organization on the dais.
    D. As the delegates reached the convention hall late, they blamed their tardiness on the taxi driver.

    17._____

18. A. The new system is superior from every point of view to the inefficient system in use until now.
    B. The reason for the strike, you may recall, was because the union demanded a closed shop.
    C. Who's to decide whether it is to be installed?
    D. To suit Mr. Knolls, the new device will have to save time, money, and the dispositions of the employees.

    18._____

19. A. Everyone can have a wonderful time in New York if they will just not try to see the entire city in one week.
    B. Being a stranger in town myself, I know how you feel.
    C. New York City is a city of man-made wonders awe-inspiring as those found in nature.
    D. He felt deep despair (as who has not?) at the evidence of man's inhumanity to man.

    19._____

20. A. In the recipe for custard, two cupfuls of milk will be enough.
    B. In the home economics classroom two tubs of clothes showed that it was not a day for cooking.
    C. It was 4:00 P.M. before the dishes were cleared away, washed, and put back into the closet.
    D. If only I had a fairy godmother like Cinderella!

21. A. The zinnia has the more vivid color, but the violet is the sweeter-smelling.
    B. About three-fourths of the review I read was merely a summary of the story; the rest, criticism.
    C. I shall insist that he not be accepted as a member, since he is very bad-tempered.
    D. No sooner had he begun to speak when his auditors started to boo and hiss.

22. A. The children's determination to find their dog almost resulted in tragedy.
    B. They spent the first night in a house that was unlocked and with no one at home.
    C. "What he asked me," said the boy, "was, 'Where can I find your father?'"
    D. It was the whimpering of a younger child and the comforting words of her brother that a member of the search-party heard about ten feet off the road.

23. A. If I would have known how extraordinarily conscientious these visitors would be, I would have prepared a more elaborate trip.
    B. Enormous purchases of millinery are not warranted by business conditions in the large cities of this country.
    C. Joan studies English, physics, history, French, and algebra.
    D. I was asked which of the two books I liked better.

24. A. When I reached the station, I discovered that I forgot my billfold.
    B. If Brutus had taken Cassius's advice, he would not have given Antony permission to speak.
    C. If John fails to help his mother, he will regret his selfishness.
    D. My father plans to visit the Philippines Islands in the fall, provided he can get accommodations on a steamer.

25. A. There was something surreptitious and sacrilegious about his conduct: I didn't care for his personality at all.
    B. Since it is liable to rain, be sure to take your umbrella with you to the game.
    C. If he could ever remember consistently where he had laid important papers, he would assume that the millenium had arrived.
    D. There is no need to engage in self-flagellation each time you make an error; to err is human.

26. A. In this cool room, neither the rose nor the gardenia will lose their freshness.
    B. Unless his persistent asceticism gets immediate psychiatric attention, the patient is very likely to find himself in a sanitarium.
    C. He has doubtless fully proven his innocence.
    D. Whether the Korean War has seriously affected the home front or not is a matter that needs further discussion.

27. A. Confectioner's sugar is frequently used in baking. 27.____
    B. What happens when an immovable object meets an irrestible force?
    C. The principle reason for his objecting to any propitiatory gestures was that he was not a person who forgets an insult easily.
    D. He was operated upon for appendicitis.

28. A. I read where the weather forecaster said a snow storm was coming. 28.____
    B. The thunder, not the flashes of lightning, frightens Janet.
    C. Harold doesn't study as I do.
    D. Thomas prefers that kind of grapes to any other on the market.

29. A. From the position of the fingerprints, the detective inferred that the man who had fired the shot was left-handed. 29.____
    B. Do you know the name of the boy who sits next to you in our music class?
    C. He spared himself much embarrassment by returning back home.
    D. How serious a matter it is to try to resist, I have had ample opportunity to observe.

30. A. My old friend and adviser is sick, I am sorry to say. 30.____
    B. Can you recall my telling you the story?
    C. He used a ten-foot pole in the pole vault, and very nearly broke the record.
    D. Obviously pleased, the assemblyman told the senator that he had been elected.

31. A. His indifferent attitude and phlegmatic temperament contributed to the candidate's defeat in the plebiscite. 31.____
    B. We reached home, but the house was completely dark and we opened the door and saw Buster wagging his tail.
    C. With leaden feet Time creeps along.
    D. Jerry asked this question: "How should the ghost be represented on the stage?"

32. A. The entire list of names of candidates was printed in the evening papers. 32.____
    B. If I should miss the train heaven forbid! I'll telephone you at once.
    C. During the current year, I have bought a new book every month.
    D. Since the bell did not ring yet, I plan to remain in the room for a while longer.

33. A. I gave a folder to everybody present, not omitting myself. 33.____
    B. I was pleased delighted, I should say to hear your excellent report.
    C. The reason I have no pen is that I lent it to my assistant.
    D. Can you ever be sure that the person whom you know is a friend of yours today will be your friend tomorrow?

34. A. Many colleges report that war veterans do work equal in quality to that of other students, or even better. 34.____
    B. I intend to be a lawyer because it is interesting work.
    C. Today the news is very disturbing, and we hear it through many avenues.
    D. How different he is from his younger brother!

35. A. In one aspect of the situation, Sam was better than any of the other men in his group; he could endure long hours, cold winds, and get drenched all day.
    B. No sooner had he entered the room than pandemonium broke loose.
    C. As a young man, I was incorrigible with respect to order; now that I am grown old, I feel very sensibly the want of it.
    D. If my father were as young as I, he would have a very different outlook on life.

36. A. Dickens' A TALE OF TWO CITIES is widely read in English classes.
    B. Give the book to whoever appeared first on line.
    C. Having borrowed over a thousand dollars, he was able to attend college for a year.
    D. 30 scientists listened in rapt attention to a succinct explanation of the function of chlorophyll.

37. A. These are the criteria for judging the merit of this composition.
    B. Aside from this error in punctuation, your composition is excellent.
    C. The sign on the road cautioned him to drive slow and to watch for children.
    D. The pupils asked permission to partake in the assembly program; however, they were refused.

38. A. He determined to enter and win the race.
    B. I find it difficult even to imagine a good excuse for his absence.
    C. Do you object to him joining us?
    D. If I were only there now, perhaps I might be able to help.

39. A. See that you attribute to no word a meaning different from the one it had a hundred years ago.
    B. No one could say for sure whether the scurrilous attack in the newspaper had brought on the cerebral hemorrhage.
    C. There were less pupils in the auditorium during the rehearsal for the school pageant than we had expected.
    D. When I saw that he wasn't working today, I realized fully the seriousness of his ailment.

40. A. When the President had finished his speech, everybody cheered; he lifted his hand in acknowledgment to them as he took his seat.
    B. I never heard of a woman's being offended by flattery.
    C. Some who have participated in military trials say it is not designed to promote justice for the defendant.
    D. Officers serving on court martial should peruse the documents with the utmost care.

41. A. Within his huge area is produced two-thirds the oats, more than half the corn, and half the wheat, wool and cotton.
    B. We can send you the refrigerator today, or we can keep it in the factory for a few days, if it is necessary to do so.
    C. Since his car is headed west, he'll not reach Maryland on that road.
    D. Never underestimate the value of a high school education.

42.
   A. All my friends were waiting when I arrived, and, despite my lateness, they greeted me courteously.
   B. He worked silently and swiftly, hoping to end his patient's discomfort quickly.
   C. Born in Salzburg, Mozart spent his childhood touring the cities of Europe.
   D. Please note the difference between "wither," "weather," "Whether," and "Whither."

42._____

43.
   A. Who did they say won?
   B. The man whom I thought was my friend deceived me.
   C. Send whoever will do the work.
   D. The question of who should be leader arose.

43._____

44.
   A. I will not go unless I receive a special invitation.
   B. The pilot shouted orders to his assistant as the plane burst into flames.
   C. She acts as though her feelings were hurt.
   D. Please come here and try and help me finish this piece of work.

44._____

45.
   A. Choose an author as you choose a friend.
   B. Home is home, be it ever so humble.
   C. You always look well in that sort of clothes.
   D. We had no sooner entered the room when the bell rung.

45._____

46.
   A. Never before, to the best of my recollection, have there been such promising students.
   B. It is only because your manners are so objectionable that you are not invited to the party.
   C. I fully expected that the children would be at their desks and to find them ready to begin work.
   D. A complete system of railroads covers the entire country.

46._____

47.
   A. The remainder of the time was spent in prayer.
   B. Immigration is when people come into a foreign country to live.
   C. He coughed continually last winter.
   D. The method is different from the one that was formerly used.

47._____

48.
   A. She is not nearly so clever as her older sister.
   B. In some ways our immediate ancestors differed but slightly from our primitive forebears.
   C. You had better pay close attention to the directions.
   D. This young cartoonist can draw as well or even better than a veteran artist.

48._____

49.
   A. Had the warden been more alert, the desperado would not have escaped so easily.
   B. "Come into my parlor," he said, "and make yourself at home."
   C. If we would have held out another week, the strike would have ended in our favor.
   D. The embattled troops rallied around that famous cry, "They shall not pass!"

49._____

50.
   A. Stroking his beard thoughtfully, an idea suddenly came to him.
   B. I read recently in an encyclopedia that Izaak Walton lived to the age of ninety.
   C. There are many reasons given for his success, his wit being most frequently mentioned.
   D. Having heard all the testimony in the case, the jury was charged by the judge.

50._____

KEY (CORRECT ANSWERS)

1. B	11. A	21. D	31. B	41. A
2. A	12. D	22. B	32. D	42. D
3. A	13. B	23. A	33. D	43. B
4. B	14. C	24. A	34. B	44. D
5. C	15. D	25. B	35. A	45. D
6. C	16. C	26. A	36. D	46. C
7. A	17. D	27. C	37. D	47. B
8. C	18. B	28. A	38. C	48. D
9. A	19. A	29. C	39. C	49. C
10. B	20. D	30. D	40. C	50. A

TEST 2

DIRECTIONS: In each of the following groups, one of the four sentences contains an error in grammar, usage, diction, or punctuation. Indicate the INCORRECT sentence. *PRINT THE LETTER OF THE CORRECT ANSWER IN THE SPACE AT THE RIGHT.*

1. A. In recent years, the metals in many articles have been substituted by plastics.
   B. They are not in Boston now, but I think they're going to that city next week.
   C. The bag of peanuts was lost.
   D. His decision was firmly stated: there would be no more excursions.

   1.____

2. A. There is, in these manifestations of distrust and suspicion, the very germ of dissension which may sprout into war.
   B. Whenever I read Somerset Maugham's OF HUMAN BONDAGE, I take a renewed interest in El Greco's art.
   C. The newest model of gun, as well as all previous models, have been made obsolete by atomic power.
   D. Neither machines nor manpower is lacking for the peaceful tasks that lie ahead.

   2.____

3. A. There was, in the first place, no indication that a crime had been committed.
   B. She is taller than any other member of her class.
   C. She decided to leave the book lay on the table.
   D. Haven't you any film in stock at the present time?

   3.____

4. A. The boys at camp liked swimming, boating, and to go on long hikes.
   B. The news of the victory was broadcast to all the soldiers in the field.
   C. He dived into the pool and swam to the opposite end.
   D. There were half a dozen people present who were attending the club's meeting for the first time.

   4.____

5. A. Located on a mountainside with a babbling brook beside the door, it was a dream palace.
   B. Blessed are they who have not seen and yet have believed.
   C. The customs in that part of the country are much different than I expected.
   D. Politics, even in towns of small population, has always attracted ambitious young lawyers.

   5.____

6. A. If John were here, he would help you solve the problem.
   B. Your statement that the report was not complete has aroused our suspicions.
   C. Every time I see you, you act like you're angry about something.
   D. Had he been your friend, he would have told you the plan.

   6.____

7. A. I'm not feeling so good, may I lie down for a few minutes?
   B. Although the second attempt was somewhat better than the first, it was far from satisfactory.
   C. I wish I could play golf as well as he.
   D. We plan to meet my brother and her at the church.

   7.____

8. A. Baseball games, which are generally noisy, should not be played on the sand lot near the hospital.
    B. Boys, who work their way through school find it difficult to visit the library.
    C. They offered the prize to the girl who had the highest average for the term.
    D. This tall, anemic girl, who is considerably younger than she appears, has been undernourished since babyhood.

9. A. She is somewhat disagreeable at home, but is always pleasant at school.
    B. During the entire night, we heard the mournful sound of the fog horn.
    C. Anyone can read the huge warning sign at the turn in the road, if they want to.
    D. The United States is a great country; its citizens should cherish its ideals of democracy.

10. A. If everyone does his duty, the plan will not fail.
    B. In the present situation, no one but I can help you.
    C. The sick man lay in bed all day, but rose in the evening to eat his dinner.
    D. I had begun to think I had lost my way, when suddenly I saw the paved highway.

11. A. Our vacation is over, I am sorry to say.
    B. It is so dark that I can't hardly see.
    C. Either you or I am right; we cannot both be right.
    D. After it had lain in the rain all night, it was not fit for use again.

12. A. The climate of New York is colder than California.
    B. I shall wait for you on the corner opposite the drug store.
    C. Here come my father and mother.
    D. Being a very modest person, John seldom talks about his invention.

13. A. My visit to Africa was fraught with untold perils.
    B. Visiting Montmartre is always an exciting adventure.
    C. Will there be a chance of you visiting Europe next year?
    D. Visiting me the other day, she explained why she had failed to leave them.

14. A. Do you remember when the late President Roosevelt said that "We have nothing to fear but fear itself?"
    B. Alas, how soon we grow forgetful of those rows of little white crosses all over the world!
    C. Mosquitoes have many larvae in stagnant pools; the best way to destroy them is to suffocate them by means of a film of oil spread over the water.
    D. "Please tell me," he politely interrupted, "whether you can spell 'Mississippi'."

15. A. If he were wealthy, he would build a hospital for the poor.
    B. I shall insist that he obey you.
    C. They believe it to be she who sent me the warning.
    D. What kind of cactus is this one?

16. A. When you go to the library tomorrow, please bring this book to the librarian in the reference room.
    B. His speech is so precise as to seem affected.
    C. I had sooner serve overseas than remain inactive at home.
    D. We read each other's letters.

17. A. John, a popular boy with many friends, was invited to spend a week at the camp. 17._____
     B. My failure was due to the poor method of study I employed at that time.
     C. When I graduated high school, I was only fifteen years old.
     D. We have a right to infer from your remarks that you think him guilty.

18. A. Ladies' hats are more expensive now than ever. 18._____
     B. They were frightened by his shrieking.
     C. They were grateful to whomever would help them.
     D. Large groups of persons visit the shrine every day.

19. A. On one side was a swamp, on the other a river. 19._____
     B. Take those books next door.
     C. Jack was running for our team when suddenly he drops the ball.
     D. The data which were used had been supplied by the agents.

20. A. Such consideration as you can give us will be appreciated. 20._____
     B. It looks to me like another World War will break out any minute.
     C. The boat sank at noon, but it was early evening before the first rescuers arrived on the spot.
     D. Microscopy is, with him, more than a fad.

21. A. Such participation, under wise leadership, has developed a sense of security and happiness in many citizens. 21._____
     B. He is here using the word "esquire" in the British sense of country gentlemen.
     C. We were sure, knowing him, that of the two alternatives, he would choose the one that was most difficult.
     D. It is true of Jim; it is true of Bill; it is true of Mary.

22. A. Neither opportunity nor ability has been absent from his career. 22._____
     B. The new era was brought about by us younger women.
     C. New York City is larger than any other city in the country.
     D. Anybody can sell this magazine in their neighborhood.

23. A. I am neither a villain, as has been alleged, or a coward. 23._____
     B. I wish I had been there when the incident occurred.
     C. He asked, "Shall you be twenty on your next birthday?"
     D. They went through all the formalities of a diplomatic function.

24. A. I can't understand Helen's making that mistake. 24._____
     B. He has lain there so long that he feels stiff all over.
     C. I don't know that we can go along.
     D. The reason why he had always avoided the honor of the Garter was because he knew that it cost a thousand pounds.

25. A. My brother detected the cause of the fire himself. 25._____
     B. Every sheet of white paper has been torn across the middle.
     C. The word "concurred" has been deleted and substituted by the word "dissented."
     D. This is a plain statement of fact endorsed by every diplomat now in Paris.

26. A. After all, consistency is the one important thing in business letter copy.
    B. I urged her to come down from off her high horse.
    C. A tattered flag hung all day from an attic window.
    D. There is nothing to puzzle you, because you don't have to send one penny or promise anything.

27. A. You are entirely right in your opinion about trespassing.
    B. He accepted the invitation because he enjoyed both fishing and to swim.
    C. All the sample books have thrilled countless readers.
    D. Getting down to brass tacks is difficult for my chief.

28. A. She objected to me reading so many novels and mystery stories.
    B. She is younger by many years than I.
    C. The ornateness of the paintings and the furnishings was not pleasing to my aesthetic sense.
    D. If you hadn't laid the book in the drawer, I should have had no difficulty in locating it.

29. A. Among the Bible stories that interest most people is the one about the battle between David and the giant, Goliath.
    B. They all arrived on time except you and I.
    C. She is so much taller than I, that I feel like a pigmy alongside her.
    D. I have always heard that the four years at college are the happiest years in a man's life.

30. A. We trusted to the sound of our footsteps on the gravel to keep us on the path.
    B. I have never been partial to those kind of newspapers.
    C. All suggestions pertaining to the improvement of conditions were considered from the standpoint of their practicability.
    D. My brother, with two of his friends, has joined the World Federalist movement.

31. A. While I was there I had many unpleasant experiences, some of which I shall never forget.
    B. Because he was independent of any political affiliation, his was a one-man campaign.
    C. The people cheered as soldier after soldier made their appearance.
    D. It is every citizen's duty first to register, and then to vote for the candidate best qualified.

32. A. The chairman, elected unanimously by the committee, has resigned.
    B. I shall give a copy of this pamphlet to whoever would like one.
    C. The boy should of completed his work the day before yesterday.
    D. Through all my troubles, I depended upon my roommate, than whom no stauncher friend exists.

33. A. Any of them is eligible to compete for the scholarship.
    B. Irregardless of your opinion, I feel inclined to be guided by my intuition.
    C. I should like everyone who I believe is capable to undertake this task.
    D. He was intent upon what he was doing and could not be distracted.

34. A. At the school at which she registered she will learn painting, dancing and to sing.   34._____
    B. Far out on the last jagged rock we could detect what appeared to be a wreck.
    C. She had, as those with strong natures always have, an unbounded confidence in her luck.
    D. Shaw made his first plunge into controversy: he rose to his feet, shaking with excitement, and heard himself speaking.

35. A. Neither the salary nor the work offers any great inducement to him.   35._____
    B. This property of my sister's is going to be sold soon.
    C. The temperature in Bermuda is almost never higher than Arizona or New Mexico.
    D. His satire on the corrupt society of the seventeenth century is subtly drawn.

36. A. Having eaten their lunch, the boat was quickly loaded and the picknickers departed.   36._____
    B. The materials were distributed among the four applicants.
    C. The man who was really responsible, the accountant, was arrested.
    D. "When did you arrive?" he asked.

37. A. The broiled fish looked good but tasted bad.   37._____
    B. The woman whom I believed to be his sister is his daughter.
    C. The last suggestion is more suitable than all that have been offered up to this point.
    D. The person who I always thought was my most dependable friend proved a great disappointment.

38. A. The scholarship was offered to whoever could show need of financial assistance.   38._____
    B. By applying himself diligently to the task, it was finally whipped into shape.
    C. This book has apparently lain undisturbed on the library shelf for many years.
    D. Weather prediction is based on data which are ascertained by means of sensitive instruments.

39. A. No answer having been received, it was assumed that Farley was no longer interested in the project.   39._____
    B. Neither the teachers nor the principal was discouraged by the results of the test.
    C. When engaged in reading, I do not like to be disturbed.
    D. Reading a few books thoughtfully is better than to skim many books superficially.

40. A. The pupil whom the faculty believed would win the essay contest failed to submit a paper.   40._____
    B. Bats are unable to see in the dark, yet avoid obstacles in a lightless cave.
    C. Luckily, none of the passengers in the wrecked plane was killed.
    D. None of Joan's class can draw more sensitively than she.

41. A. The rapid growth of television cannot but affect other media of mass entertainment.   41._____
    B. As a health resort, the high, dry air of the Rockies is always recommended for people suffering from lung trouble.
    C. Each of the children was given two teaspoonfuls of cod liver oil.
    D. "Ask Mr. Esposito," said Tom; "perhaps he can tell you."

42. A. The results of his investigations he embodied in three of the most brilliant essays he or any other Harvard graduate ever wrote.
    B. Whatever the consequences, my decision is irrevocable.
    C. If Barbara would have thought twice, she would not have spoken as she did.
    D. I think that you'll agree with me that CHARLOTTE'S WEB is one of the best children's books that have been published this year.

43. A. Mozart's chamber music, as well as his operas, are delightful to hear.
    B. The producer reported that he had recently read the revised third act and thought it excellent.
    C. Nobody but James and him was able to go to the Planetarium.
    D. The chimes rang true and sweet and gladdened the hearts of the listeners.

44. A. "Why," asked the magistrate, "did you pass the red light?"
    B. Respect for others, loyalty, integrity—these are the essential ingredients of good character.
    C. Be only satisfied with the best.
    D. If I were able to play a musical instrument, I should be very happy.

45. A. Doctors say that certain throat conditions are aggravated by smoking.
    B. When I hear someone speak of their thirteenth year as an unlucky year, I am irritated by the persistence of superstition.
    C. There are no words in English in which two c's follow the prefix re.
    D. Sir Toby Belch—he is the clown in TWELFTH NIGHT—is one of Shakespeare's most vivid characters.

46. A. The men's department is on the fifth floor, while the boys' is on the fourth.
    B. It was she whom the policeman had warned to remain on the sidewalk.
    C. Into every life come both joy and sorrow.
    D. The carton contained these items; a loaf of bread, a compass, a tattered diary, and a pair of muddy shoes.

47. A. The fact that Jones and Company reduced the amount of it's employees is no indication that there is a slump.
    B. I saw Mrs. Brown, her whom you pointed out at the meeting.
    C. John, that suit looks unusually good on you.
    D. We know the culprits to be them.

48. A. I don't see why he should feel so bad about his loss; its not as though he were impoverished.
    B. If he was honest, he would return the money.
    C. But for his uncle's intervention he would have been discharged.
    D. think they, on the average, are much heavier than we.

49. A. Conditions here are much better than Europe.
    B. The study of the changes that have taken place and the reasons for them is fascinating.
    C. I found the play exciting (and frightening), but the audience seemed unmoved by it.
    D. Neither of the boys was willing to go.

50. A. The lazy pupil, of course, will tend to write the minimum amount of words acceptable.
    B. The proposal that we should all go together was accepted enthusiastically.
    C. Had you heard the argument, you would be ready to excuse his anger.
    D. Dickens wrote DAVID COPPERFIELD; Thackeray, VANITY FAIR.

50.____

KEY (CORRECT ANSWERS)

1.	A	11.	B	21.	C	31.	C	41.	B
2.	C	12.	A	22.	D	32.	C	42.	C
3.	C	13.	C	23.	A	33.	B	43.	A
4.	A	14.	A	24.	D	34.	A	44.	C
5.	C	15.	C	25.	C	35.	C	45.	B
6.	C	16.	A	26.	B	36.	A	46.	D
7.	A	17.	C	27.	B	37.	C	47.	A
8.	B	18.	C	28.	A	38.	B	48.	B
9.	C	19.	C	29.	B	39.	D	49.	A
10.	B	20.	B	30.	B	40.	A	50.	A

EXAMINATION SECTION
TEST 1

DIRECTIONS: In each of the following groups of sentences, there are three sentences which are correct and one which is incorrect because it contains an error in grammar, usage, diction, or punctuation. Indicate the INCORRECT sentence. *PRINT THE LETTER OF THE CORRECT ANSWER IN THE SPACE AT THE RIGHT.*

1. A. Take one of these books which are to be discarded because it has no value any more.
   B. Although the period has lasted for more than thirty minutes, the students are not tired and can do much more work.
   C. Williams has a most unique idea for the school play, and he plans to discuss it with his teacher.
   D. After cleaning the house, my mother lay in the hammock for an hour; then she went shopping.

   1.____

2. A. Sunrise High School, with an enrollment of 1,200 boys and 1,100 girls, is the largest in the state.
   B. I was pleased with his visiting me in the hospital as I was lonely and depressed at the time.
   C. To type with your feet spread out in all directions is considered to be an example of poor typewriting technique.
   D. First-class furs like first-class diamonds are very expensive; both the initial cost and the year-to-year upkeep require a great deal of money.

   2.____

3. A. Not having received a reply to my letter of June 8, I am writing again to ask if anything is wrong.
   B. She asked, "Whom does Mr. Jones feel should have won the typewriting medal?"
   C. Strawberries and cream is a perfect summer dessert, and I have asked my mother to serve the dish frequently.
   D. Either Mary or the boys have broken the window, and I mean to find out immediately before they do further damage.

   3.____

4. A. Of the ladies present at the meeting, three were chosen to be delegates to the annual convention to be held the following May.
   B. The reason I succeeded is that I prepared thoroughly for the test.
   C. I heard her say that the window was broken by the ball and damaged the vase in the living room.
   D. They have been chosen for two reasons—namely, because they are intelligent and because they are conscientious.

   4.____

5. A. Latin, French, and English, in that order, were my favorite subjects in high school.
   B. Since a stay of execution has not been received from the governor, the murderer must be hanged at midnight.
   C. Knowing that you want an immediate answer, I suggest that you send your request to Mr. Smith or to whoever is in charge of such matters.
   D. We ordered pencils and typewriter ribbons whichever were available from the stationer on the corner.

   5.____

117

6. A. Business was not good; and becoming very irritated, the partners decided to close the store for the day.
    B. I am pleased with your work — work that shows through preparation and in your typewriting ability.
    C. The house was low and long and appeared to be newly built.
    D. This office is often used by salesmen who have nothing better to do, and especially by unsuccessful salesmen.

6.___

7. A. Reading this well-written book was a never-to-be forgotten experience; I was both repelled and drawn toward the hero.
    B. I can hardly realize that in two weeks I shall be in Europe. The reason is that I have never traveled before.
    C. I want four only, but I will take five or six if you insist.
    D. Mrs. Jones plans to speak with Sally about her poor grades. The girl failed two subjects last month.

7.___

8. A. Strictly speaking, he cannot be considered a good base ball player — or, for that matter, a good tennis player.
    B. To learn to type well, you should practice daily; to acquire high speed in shorthand, you should practice constantly.
    C. The teachers' committee consisted of Dr. Smith, the principal, Mr. Jones, the program committee chairman, Mrs. Greene, the senior grade adviser, and the administrative assistant.
    D. His secretary and Girl Friday was the most efficient worker he had ever hired, and he was delighted with her.

8.___

9. A. There were but two of us left after examinations had been graded.
    B. Neither the two bushes nor the elm tree was damaged by the hurricane.
    C. "Did you go to the office?", Mary asked. "No," Sally replied, "and I don't intend to."
    D. The engine as well as the fenders and the wheels was severely damaged, and neither you nor I am prepared to say how much the repair bill will be.

9.___

10. A. I observed that the house was one of those rambling old mansions that one often sees in Southern towns.
    B. By concentrating on spelling while I am learning how to type, I am putting my time to better use.
    C. Please repeat the sentence again because none of the children in the rear heard you.
    D. The police have arrested three men: John Winters, 27, Brooklyn; Timothy Flynn, 26, Brooklyn; and Sheldon Young, 26, Queens.

10.___

11. A. "I have laid the book down," she said. "I shall now go to sleep."
    B. The policeman, not the gangsters, merits our approval despite the fact that crime is made to be so attractive on television.
    C. "Did you finish your composition yet?" Sally asked. "No," Jane replied.
    D. Where can I find out who wrote, "What you don't know would make a great book"?

11.___

12. A. I read in a book that boys and girls today are taller and heavier than their parents were at the same age. How interesting!
    B. John said that from where he was sitting in the ball park, he could hardly see the batter and the pitcher.
    C. He expects to be graduated from Morningside High School in January instead of June as he has been taking extra summer courses.
    D. Speaking of employment, have many new jobs been created on Long Island as a result of all the industries which have settled there during the past five years?

13. A. I have risen at five o'clock in the morning for the past twenty years, and I am still in excellent physical condition.
    B. I have laid the letter on my employer's desk several times, but he still has not signed it.
    C. We felt that if he would have tried harder, he might have passed the examination.
    D. I am angry with John principally because I am angry at the comments he made at the rally last night.

14. A. I met a friend of father's the other day in Boland and Ryan's suburban store.
    B. Less men were hurt this year than last because of the intensive safety precautions which have been introduced.
    C. During several months — that is, June, July, and August — school is closed.
    D. We need all types of skills in our office — for example stenographers, typists, IBM operators, duplicator operators, and typist-clerks.

15. A. The paper says that civil liberties is the principal topic of conversation in Washington today.
    B. I do not know why — but perhaps I shouldn't try to find out at this time.
    C. I would have preferred to do nothing until he came, so I decided to lie down.
    D. As I was entering the office, I heard a bell clang right behind me, which gave me a bad fright.

16. A. As I went deeper and deeper into the forest, the light became dimmer and dimmer.
    B. Did he actually say, "I can't do a thing for you"? I can imagine him being so ungrateful.
    C. After he had seen the play OKLAHOMA (which he had been told in advance was excellent), he decided to go to the theater much more often.
    D. Bill Carlton did not go to college, which shocked his family and astonished his friends because Bill was a really good student.

17. A. If Tom had worked all summer in a camp or in a restaurant, he might have saved enough money to buy a car.
    B. I am not sure which typewriter is liked better, the Royal or the IBM Selectric; and I plan, therefore, to look into the matter further.
    C. We stopped at John's house to see if his trophy was different from Mark's trophy.
    D. Tom said that he was going over to Sally's house after the school dance and that we should not expect him home until midnight.

18. A. Tom never has and never will obtain the grades required for admission to Harvard.   18.___
    B. The rain fell harder and harder as I walked away from home.
    C. "There is nothing to worry about dear," her mother answered quietly. "What a fuss you do get into! Heavens! Now take the nice medicine."
    D. The union leader, whom it was believed all the men admired, was, in fact, very much hated by most of them.

19. A. You had better not stay too long or you will get into trouble—unless, of course, you just don't care.   19.___
    B. His latest book The Psychology of Mental Life was published in 1991. Have you read his other books?
    C. The clerk whom I thought to be the best was, in actuality, the worst.
    D. He said that he sold: typewriters, adding machines, mail equipment, and time clocks.

20. A. There was danger of the enemy attacking from the rear and destroying our army before we could bring up the necessary reserves.   20.___
    B. There were approximately ten applicants in the office waiting to be interviewed for the job.
    C. He acts, it seems to me, as though he were guilty.
    D. We have studied John Smith's, William Wilson's, and Tom Blake's claims; and we feel quite sure that they will soon be settled.

21. A. He is a person who pleases you the moment you meet him, so that you want to be with him and to know him better.   21.___
    B. He had no love for, nor confidence in, his employer.
    C. First type the letter and then you should put it in the envelope.
    D. His salary was lower than a typist's, but he did not care because there were excellent opportunities for advancement.

22. A. I typed this letter – you may not believe this, but it is true – in four minutes.   22.___
    B. "It is clear (the message read) that the Muscle Shoals development is but a small part of the potential public usefulness of the entire Tennessee River."–D.E. Lilienthal
    C. Shaw made his first plunge into controversy: he rose to his feet, shaking with nerves and heard himself speaking.
    D. After the reading of the will, he opened up the strong box and divided up the money among the relatives present.

23. A. Dissatisfaction with the theoretical bases and practical workings of the general property tax has given rise to two movements of tax reform.   23.___
    B. Let the book lie on the table.
    C. Since the department is reducing its number of employees is not proof that they are not needed.
    D. Who do you think will be selected for the position?

24. A. Application of the principles discovered during those experiments have been of great value to mankind.   24.___
    B. Every one of the editorial assistants proved his worth without exception.
    C. State regulation of morals aids in the protection of the family.
    D. Working when one is tired does not yield the best results.

25. A. We learned that there was more than ten people present at the conference.
    B. Every one of the employees is able to lift the carton.
    C. Neither the registrar nor the secretary is in the office today.
    D. The administrative assistant stated that any office assistant who stayed overtime tonight would get a half-day off next month.

25._____

KEY (CORRECT ANSWERS)

1.	C		11.	C
2.	D		12.	B
3.	B		13.	C
4.	C		14.	B
5.	D		15.	D
6.	B		16.	B
7.	A		17.	D
8.	C		18.	A
9.	C		19.	D
10.	C		20.	A

21.	C
22.	D
23.	C
24.	A
25.	A

TEST 2

DIRECTIONS: In each of the following groups of sentences, there are three sentences which are correct and one which is incorrect because it contains an error in grammar, usage, diction, or punctuation. Indicate the INCORRECT sentence. *PRINT THE LETTER OF THE CORRECT ANSWER IN THE SPACE AT THE RIGHT.*

1. A. I read political science books as a kind of a duty, not for pleasure. 1.___
   B. You needn't go to all that expense for me.
   C. It will be extremely interesting to note the varied reactions of the other participants.
   D. Please do not be angry with me, because it really was not my fault.

2. A. We go there by boat and return by train. 2.___
   B. He wrote home for his bathing trunks, tennis racket, and set of golf clubs.
   C. Take me to his home, and I will tell him myself.
   D. The autobiography of George Bernard Shaw by Ernest Jones was assigned for reading by my English teacher.

3. A. Everyone was given his fair share. 3.___
   B. If the river will rise much higher, we may have a flood.
   C. There were, in the early years of this century, many more horses than automobiles.
   D. Either your enunciation is faulty or I am hard of hearing.

4. A. The boy assured his teacher that he would pass the tests with ease. 4.___
   B. Every person in these two buildings has to meet their responsibilities.
   C. Thunderstorms will invariably follow a lengthy hot spell.
   D. I believe the boy to be him.

5. A. I lay it on the bench before I left. 5.___
   B. She wrung the clothes before she bought a washing machine.
   C. We have drunk all the water.
   D. The wind has blown like this all night.

6. A. I like Shakespeare's HAMLET better than any of his plays. 6.___
   B. The roads are in poor condition because of the torrential rains.
   C. They robbed the child.
   D. They have stolen my cash.

7. A. If the winner of the contest were here, I would give him his medal. 7.___
   B. I hope my son graduates junior high school next June.
   C. Now is the time to make sure that we have beaten that team.
   D. We believe that those books are up to date.

8. A. Be careful that you do not slip on that oily surface. 8.___
   B. I hope to be able to take notes during his worthwhile lecture.
   C. I think that phenomena is worth photographing.
   D. It occurred in the 1960s, not during the 1950s.

9. A. New York is larger than any city in Europe.
   B. Just as we reached the boat landing, the weather changed.
   C. Coming around the curve, the large house was seen.
   D. Generally speaking, my daughter is a good student.

9.____

10. A. Place the children's toys above the others.
    B. It was more unique that I thought it would be.
    C. It was my opinion, albeit an erroneous one, that he was the best swimmer on the team.
    D. The typewriter's ribbon was frayed.

10.____

11. A. The chances are that Ted's relatives believe in his honesty.
    B. I am glad that you think this was so.
    C. Give it to the club to which my grandmother belongs.
    D. I am in New York for ten years.

11.____

12. A. I have heard that he is never returning.
    B. In the last century it was especially fashionable to dress in that manner.
    C. This data, in my opinion, is incorrect.
    D. It is a highly selective procedure which must be followed.

12.____

13. A. She sat besides me on the couch.
    B. Billy is the best Spanish scholar of the three boys.
    C. It is gratifying to know that the city school system's strengths are being publicized.
    D. I do not have very much faith in his changing his mind.

13.____

14. A. I think that he should be feeling somewhat better.
    B. Do as she does if you want to do it correctly.
    C. I am surely glad that he was able to pass the test.
    D. Hide it some place.

14.____

15. A. He seemed to be possessed by an evil spirit.
    B. I think that his point of view is different from mine, but I still believe that I am correct.
    C. I agree to the new plan, but I disagree with him in regard to how it is to be accomplished.
    D. He has the natural desire to be independent from his parents.

15.____

16. A. Whenever she went to school she learned a lot.
    B. We had hoped to be on time, but we were late.
    C. My greatest fear, however, was overcome at the last moment.
    D. The two painters' works were displayed at the gallery.

16.____

17. A. The check from the Treasury Department will arrive on Monday, January 23.
    B. James was not sure that it was Jane and me at the party.
    C. I do not know if the search for William and her has been made.
    D. There were many accidents on the highway, but the toll was less than had been anticipated.

17.____

18. A. A baby girl was just what we wanted.
    B. His vote was the larger of the two candidates.
    C. That boy had neither money or influence, and I do not know what chances of success he had.
    D. I may lie down on that bed if I get tired.

18.___

19. A. He doesn't live too far from his friend's home.
    B. The northeast was covered with snow.
    C. Let's cut it into six portions so that we can each have a piece.
    D. The boy did six days' work.

19.___

20. A. It was in first-class condition, and I decided to keep it.
    B. It was a highly polished piece of jewelry.
    C. The twins, not their little brother, has the measles.
    D. That is the most important document in the history of our country.

20.___

21. A. Medical training in Greece has been modernized, and the younger doctors have either studied in the United States or Europe.
    B. He will not bring the car here without my telling him.
    C. He is as tall as, if not taller than, the teacher,
    D. If one is asked to count from one to five inclusive, he should count as follows: one, two, three, four, five.

21.___

22. A. The leader of the movement is Mr. Harold L. Parne, Esq.
    B. He expects to be graduated from college next month.
    C. If one lives in Florida one day and in Iceland the next, he is certain to feel the change in temperature.
    D. He is the one of the boys who is always on time.

22.___

23. A. Since only one in the jury responded to the foreman's question, he looked at them inquiringly.
    B. According to an old adage, every dog has its day.
    C. It was I whom he wanted to sing.
    D. Now that the stress of examinations and interviews are over, we can all relax for a while.

23.___

24. A. The arrival of the letter was prior to that of the package.
    B. If you convey this suggestion back to your committee, we shall obtain a solution to our problem.
    C. They all looked different after their return from Vietnam.
    D. Illiteracy is the condition of the man who cannot read or write.

24.___

25. A. Do you think we have paid too much? too little?
    B. Neither John nor I am to receive the reward.
    C. The farmer lost nearly one hundred cattle in the fire.
    D. We are making fewer mistakes with the new calculating machine.

25.___

KEY (CORRECT ANSWERS)

1. A
2. D
3. B
4. B
5. A

6. A
7. B
8. C
9. C
10. B

11. D
12. C
13. A
14. D
15. D

16. A
17. B
18. C
19. B
20. C

21. A
22. A
23. D
24. B
25. A

TEST 3

DIRECTIONS: In each of the following groups of sentences, one sentence is incorrect because it includes an error in grammar, usage, sentence structure, capitalization, diction, or punctuation. Indicate the INCORRECT sentence. *PRINT THE LETTER OF THE CORRECT ANSWER IN THE SPACE AT THE RIGHT.*

1.
   A. Her poor posture made taking dictation a fatiguing chore.
   B. The secretary promptly notified the principal of the fire for which she was highly praised.
   C. She makes too frequent use of correction fluid when she types stencils.
   D. Old records are sometimes kept in a basement storeroom.

   1.___

2.
   A. She learned the uses of punctuation marks from one of the dictionary's appendixes.
   B. The administrative assistant acted as principal in the latter's absence.
   C. You see, you did mail the letter to yourself!
   D. We are impressed by her exemplary performance and industry; they are a stimulant to us to do better work.

   2.___

3.
   A. The rotation of duties and responsibilities among the secretaries are highly desirable.
   B. The school secretary must remember to maintain contact with teachers assigned to the Board of Education.
   C. She could not operate the electric typewriter because she had not plugged it in.
   D. Eleanor utilized a postal scale to determine the cost of mailing the parcel.

   3.___

4.
   A. Please list the names of alumnae from the year 1963 on.
   B. Her filing went like clockwork because of the prior alphabetizing of the folders.
   C. She let the phone ring for awhile, but when she finally answered, the line was dead.
   D. The secretary's merits were duly noted in the principal's report.

   4.___

5.
   A. At closing time, one should not be short tempered with long-winded visitors.
   B. The eraser was lost after it had lain alongside the typewriter.
   C. Her spelling was as acceptable as theirs, if not more acceptable.
   D. We ordered many copies of Webster's new International dictionary from federal funds.

   5.___

6.
   A. For the sake of expediency, we divided the work between the four of us.
   B. She quickly learnt to use a comptometer.
   C. Miss Smith would rather take dictation than operate the switchboard.
   D. The dimensions of the envelope determine the quantity of matter that may be enclosed.

   6.___

7.
   A. Joan's suggestion for recording absences, though untried, seems practicable.
   B. The expression, "Thanking you in advance," is unacceptable in up-to-date correspondence.
   C. She informed latecomers not to feel badly because the snowstorm would be accepted as a valid excuse.
   D. The school secretary was pleased that the courses she had taken were relevant to her work.

   7.___

8. A. He was extremely kind to me yesterday.
    B. I talked to him in regard to the subscription.
    C. They were so good to me.
    D. The teacher spoke clear and emphatic.

8.____

9. A. Our vacation is over, I am sorry to say.
    B. It is so dark that I can't hardly see.
    C. Either you or I am right; we cannot both be right.
    D. After it had lain in the rain all night, it was not fit for use again.

9.____

10. A. When either or both habits become fixed, the student improves.
    B. Neither his words nor his action was justifiable.
    C. A calm almost always comes before a storm.
    D. The gallery with all its pictures were destroyed.

10.____

11. A. Next summer I shall either travel by plane or by boat down to Bermuda.
    B. The reason Tom won the award is that he studied hard.
    C. Undoubtedly the best scene in the play occurs when the son confronts his mother.
    D. History is the record of events that have happened.

11.____

12. A. John was invited to spend a week at the camp.
    B. My failure was due to the poor method of study I employed at that time.
    C. When I left home, I was only fifteen years old.
    D. We imply from your remarks that you think him guilty.

12.____

13. A. The advantages of such an arrangement enables the teachers to plan her work more efficiently.
    B. Typing skill is the result merely of the acquisition of a number of habits.
    C. We are more likely to catch cold in overheated rooms than in chilly ones.
    D. Both political parties promise to balance the budget if and when they are elected to office.

13.____

14. A. They have neither the patience nor the skill necessary to solve these problems.
    B. This is the only decision that can be reached: either you or I are right.
    C. You should lend your book to the student who you think will enjoy reading it.
    D. The Red Cross is doing its utmost to provide medical supplies for the flood areas.

14.____

15. A. The driver sustained internal injuries.
    B. It is the only textbook of its kind that has, is, or may be published.
    C. Thinking speaking and writing are closely related learnings.
    D. Most of us recognize good English when we hear it or read it.

15.____

16. A. This sort of emergency always has its exciting moments.
    B. A tragic play is when the action ends unhappily.
    C. The committee adjourned sine die and went to their homes for a much needed rest.
    D. It is essential that you be on the alert at all times.

16.____

17. A. The reason he was late getting to work was because he overslept.
    B. As we read the daily newspaper headlines, a feeling of despair overwhelms us.
    C. His gentle speech is no proof that he is kind.
    D. Shall we lay the book on the table?

18. A. We want to travel extensively and have new experiences.
    B. Charles is my brother, James being my cousin.
    C. His teacher is one person in whom he can confide.
    D. The skater suddenly lost control and crashed into the rail.

19. A. Because he was sympathetic and tolerant, most people respected him.
    B. What are the principal points to be emphasized in the conduct of drill practice?
    C. The lecturer called attention to the beginning of the movement and how it ended.
    D. The average citizen has far more civic power than he realizes.

20. A. The committee has done their best to raise the money necessary to build the new club house.
    B. He was neither willing nor able to pay the exorbitant fee.
    C. We all want to be happy, and we want our fellow men to be happy.
    D. If ours were a totalitarian society, we would probably limit the number of pupils admitted to colleges.

21. A. The filling-out of the application blank took up one third of his time.
    B. The talent for brevity is given to few politicians!
    C. Dashing to the front window, the parade came into view.
    D. Each day this newspaper prints a summary of up-to-the-minute news on the front page.

22. A. Because of his ability as a leader, he was undoubtedly the man for the job.
    B. Not only were they disappointed but also angry.
    C. If one is to learn French well one must speak it regularly.
    D. The most famous collection of prayers known to history is the Book of Psalms.

23. A. We planned to stay a week in at Rocky Landing.
    B. The bus driver agreed to take as many as wanted to go.
    C. Any man may vote, be he rich or poor.
    D. The teacher assigned three of us, John, Sam, and I, to help with the arrangements for the party.

24. A. Today, more then ever, we need the steadying influence of stable homes and families.
    B. Was ever a man so tormented!
    C. This report — may it never be forgotten — is our last, our very last.
    D. The letter states, "I am agin(sic) every idea you have."

25. A. Although he must have known the answer, he refused to volunteer the information.
    B. The pirate captain divided up the booty among his crew according to their rank.
    C. As the gale gathered force, the captain mounted the bridge.
    D. As he threw the line over the side of the boat, he suddenly remembered that the rope was fouled.

KEY (CORRECT ANSWERS)

1. B
2. D
3. A
4. C
5. D

6. A
7. C
8. D
9. B
10. D

11. A
12. D
13. A
14. B
15. B

16. B
17. A
18. B
19. C
20. A

21. C
22. B
23. D
24. A
25. B

———

ENGLISH GRAMMAR AND USAGE

This section provides a brief review of some of the basic rules of English Usage (grammar, syntax punctuation, spelling, and organization of paragraphs in a passage).

Some *Basic English Usage Topics What is Grammar*

Grammar is the entire body of rules that governs the correct speaking and writing of a language. **Syntax** is that part of grammar that deals with the arrangement of words, phrases, and clauses within a sentence. **Punctuation** deals with the proper use of such things as commas, periods, apostrophes, and question marks which separate words into sentences, clauses, and phrases in order to clarify their meaning.

Sentence Construction

- A sentence is a grammatically independent group of words that serves as a unit of expression. It normally contains a subject and predicate.

Basic Parts of *a Simple Sentence*

- A simple sentence contains a subject, a verb, and an object.

Use of *Phrases in Sentences*

- A phrase is a group of related words lacking both subject and predicate. A phrase can be used as a noun, adjective, adverb, or verb. On the basis of their form, phrases are classified as *prepositional, participial, gerund, infinitive,* and *verb* phrases.

- A restrictive phrase (not set off by commas in the sentence) completes the meaning of the sentence. A nonrestrictive phrase (set off by commas in the sentence) is incidental to the meaning of the sentence.

Use of *Clauses in Sentences*

- Clauses are grammatical units containing a subject and a verb. They can be either dependent or independent. An independent clause expresses the main thought of the sentence. A dependent clause expresses an idea that is less important than the idea expressed in the main clause. Dependent clauses can be restrictive (not set off by commas in the sentence) or nonrestrictive (set off by commas in the sentence).

Verb

Definition: A word or phrase used to assert an action or state of being.

Voice of *Verb*

- The *voice* of a verb shows whether the subject performs an action (active voice) or receives it (passive voice). **Examples:** The consultant wrote a proposal. The proposal was written by the consultant.

Verb Tense

- The tense of a verb shows the time of the action of the verb. There is an active and a passive form of all tenses in English. The tenses of verbs in English are:
  a. Present (active) - she takes *or* she is taking
  b. Present (passive) -she is taken *or* she is being taken
  c. Past (active) - she took *or* she was taking
  d. Past (passive) -she was taken *or* she was being taken
  e. Future (active) -she will take *or* she will be taking
  f. Future (passive) -she will be taken
  g. Perfect (active) - she has taken *or* she has been taking
  h. Perfect (passive) - she has been taken
  i. Past perfect (active) - she had taken *or* she had been taking
  j. Past perfect (passive) -she had been taken
  k. Future perfect (active) - she will have taken *or* she will have been taking
  l. Future perfect (passive) - she will have been taken

Mood of the Verb

- The mood of a verb shows whether an action is fact (indicative mood), something other than fact, such as a possibility, wish, or supposition (subjunctive mood), or a command (imperative mood).
  Example of indicative mood: They are going to the ball game.
  Example of subjunctive mood: If they go at all, they will be late.
  Example of imperative mood: Go now!

Verb Shifts

- Unnecessary shifts in person, number, tense, or voice confuse readers and seriously weakens communication. The examples below indicate these types of errors.

- A shift in person occurs when a writer shifts back and forth among the first, second, and third persons. **Example:** If you want to pass the physical, a person has to exercise daily.

- A shift in number occurs when a plural pronoun is used to refer back to a singular antecedent or vice versa. **Example:** Anyone who shops in that department store must seriously consider their budget.

- Unnecessary shifts in tense more commonly occur within a paragraph rather than within an individual sentence. **Example:** After the historian spent several hours describing the armies' strategies, he gave a horrifying account of the attack. He points out in great detail what is going on in the minds of each of the soldiers.

- A shift in voice occurs when a writer makes unnecessary shifts between the active and the passive voice. **Example:** I wrote the journal article; the book chapter was also written by me. (The *voice* of a verb shows whether the subject performs an action (active voice) or receives it (passive voice).) In the example, the first clause is active voice and the second shifts to passive voice.

Other Rules Related to Verbs

- Transitive verbs require objects to complete their meaning. **Example:** The baseball player *signed the* autographs.

- Intransitive verbs do not require objects to complete their meaning. **Example:** The boat *has docked*.

- Linking verbs are not action verbs; rather, they express a state of being or existence. The various forms of the verb *to be* are primary linking verbs.

- Linking verbs never take objects but, instead, connect the subject to a word or idea in the predicate. **Examples:** It was he who bought the tickets. His proposal *is* unacceptable. Some dogs *are* excitable.

- The verb *to be* can also be used with another verb as a helping (auxiliary) verb to create a verb phrase. Examples: Flights *have been delayed*. The contract will *have to be reviewed*

Infinitive

Definition: An infinitive is the form of a verb which expresses action or existence without reference to person, number, or tense. **Example:** *To run* is relaxing.

- A split infinitive has a word or several words between the *to* and the *verb* following it. Splitting an infinitive is incorrect. **Example:** We will try *to successfully complete this project.* **Correct Usage:** We will try to complete this project successfully.

- An infinitive may be used as the subject of a sentence. **Example:** *To become* champion has been her lifelong dream.

- An infinitive may be used as an adjectival modifier. **Example:** She had several papers *to review* during the trip.

Gerund

Definition: A gerund is the form of a verb ending in *ing* that is used as a noun. In fact, another name for a gerund is a verbal noun.

- A gerund may be used as the subject of a sentence. **Example:** *Drawing* was his favorite personal activity.

- A gerund may be used as the object of a sentence or a prepositional phrase. **Examples:** She preferred *walking* over *bicycling*. *Walking* is the object and *bicycling* is the object of the preposition *over*.

Participle

Definition: A participle is a form of the verb used as an adjective. Simple participle forms end in "_ed" or "_ing." **Examples:** The candidate felt defrayed The New Year's Eve party was *exciting*.

- When a participial phrase seems to modify a word that it cannot sensibly modify, then it is a dangling phrase. **Example:** Sailing on the open sea, many dolphins were spotted. *Sailing* does not modify dolphins. The correct use of the participle is the following: Sailing on the open sea, we spotted many dolphins.

Noun

Definition: A noun is a word that names a person, place, thing, quality, idea, or action.

- A common noun identifies one or more of a class of persons, places, things, qualities, ideas, or actions that are alike. **Examples:** The *boy* chained his *bicycle* to the *fence*.

- A proper noun identifies a particular person, place, thing, quality, idea, or action. *(Note:* needs to be capitalized.) **Examples:** *Joe Brown* drove his *Lincoln Towncar* to the *Kennedy Center.*

- A collective noun identifies a group of people or things that are related or acting as one. **Examples:** The *jury* arrives at the courthouse each day at nine in the morning. The *platoon* travels by night in order to avoid detection. *(Note:* Collective nouns are *single* in number which is reflected in the verb agreement.)

- The possessive of a singular noun is formed by adding an apostrophe and s ('s) to the noun. **Examples:** the boy's sweater; Robert's book; Alice's dress (correct) the boys' sweater; Roberts' book; Alices' dress (incorrect)

- The possessive of a plural noun ending in s is formed by adding an apostrophe only. **Examples:** wives' salaries; workers' union (correct);
  wive's salaries; worker's union (incorrect)

Pronoun

Definition: A pronoun is a word that is used in place of a noun, most frequently to eliminate monotonous repetition of the noun. There are nine types of pronouns:

- Demonstrative pronouns point out a specific person or thing. **Examples:** this, that, these, those

- Indefinite pronouns refer to people or things generally rather than specifically. Examples: all, any, anybody, anyone, anything, both, each, either, everybody, everyone, everything, few, many, most, much, neither, no one, nobody, none, nothing, one, other, several, some, somebody, someone, something, such. *(Note:* Verbs used with indefinite pronouns must agree in number. **Examples:** none *is;* much *is;* everyone *is;* many *are*. *None* and *much* are often used incorrectly to represent plural entities. If you think of *none* as *no one person or thing* and *much* as *a large quantity of one thing,* then it is easy to see that they are actually singular and take a singular verb.)
  Examples: None of the pencils is free (translates as: *no one pencil is free*) (correct)
  None of the books are listed (translates as: *no one book are listed*) (incorrect)

- Interrogative pronouns are used to ask questions. Examples: who, what, which

- Relative pronouns relate a subordinate part of a sentence to the main clause. **Examples:** who, whoever, whom, whomever, whose, which, whichever, what, whatever, that *(Note: Who* and *whoever* are used as subjects in a sentence or phrase, while *whom* and *whomever are* used as objects in a sentence or phrase.

  Examples: *Who will* get the tickets? *Whoever is* going will buy the tickets. I need to give tickets to *whom? The tickets will be given to whomever.)*

- Personal pronouns refer to persons or things and change form in three different persons: first person (the person speaking), second person (the person spoken to), and third person (the person or thing spoken about). **Examples:** I, me, we, us, you, he, him, she, her, it, they, them Examples of correct use: Bill and I are going. He told Sally and me. **Example of incorrect use:** He told Sally and I to take a break.

- Possessive pronouns determine ownership or possession without using an apostrophe followed by an s. **Examples:** my, mine, our, ours, yours, his, hers, its, their, theirs (Note: *it's* is not a personal pronoun and means *it is. There* is not a personal pronoun and refers to a location.)

- Reciprocal pronouns are used together and each can be replaced by the other. **Examples:** *each other, one another*

- Reflexive pronouns refer back to the pronoun used as the subject of the sentence. **Examples:** I burned *myself.* You are deceiving *yourself.*

- Intensive pronouns are used to emphasize the first pronoun. **Examples:** You *yourself* must register. I *myself* do not understand.

Adjective and Adverb

Definitions: An adjective is a word that modifies a noun. An adverb is a word that modifies a verb, an adjective, or another adverb.

- An adjective or an adverb should be placed so that there is no doubt as to which word it modifies. Example: The *angry* boy *quickly* threw the ball. *Angry* is an adjective modifying the noun *boy. Quickly* is an adverb modifying the verb *threw.*

- Adjectives and adverbs show degrees of quality or quantity by means of their positive, comparative, and superlative forms. The positive form expresses no comparison at all. The comparative form adds an *er* to the positive form of the adjective or adverb or prefixes the positive form with the word *more* to express a greater degree or a comparison. The superlative form adds an *est* to the positive form of the adjective or adverb or prefixes the positive form with the word *most* to express the greatest degree of quantity or quality among three or more persons or things.

Examples:	**Positive**	**Comparative**	**Superlative**
	short	shorter	shortest
	beautiful	more beautiful	most beautiful
	big	bigger	biggest
	hard	harder	hardest

- Many adverbs have the characteristic *-ly* ending. **Example:** quickly, slowly, angrily

Preposition

Definition: A preposition is a word that connects a noun to some other word in the sentence. It usually establishes a relationship of time or location. The use of a preposition automatically creates a prepositional phrase. **Examples:** in a month; after a year; on the table; behind the door

- There are over 40 prepositions in English, some of which are: *about, around, before, at, below, by, for, from, in, of, on, to, through, up, upon,* and *with.*

Conjunction

Definition: A conjunction (also known as a connective) is a word that joins together sentences, clauses, phrases, or words. Conjunctions that connect two or more parts of a sentence that are of equal rank (Example: two nouns or verbs or phrases) are called coordinating conjunctions. **Examples:** *and, but, or, nor, for,* and sometimes *yet*

- Subordinating conjunctions connect dependent (subordinate) clauses to independent (main) clauses. Subordinating conjunctions include *though, as, when, while, and since.* **Example:** *Since he took the course for his own advancement,* they wouldn't pay for it.

- Conjunctions in the forms of pairs of words that connect sentence elements that are of equal rank are called correlative conjunctions. Correlative conjunctions must always appear together in the same sentence. **Examples:** *either-or, neither-nor, whether-or, both-and,* and *not only-but also* **Examples used in sentences:** His parents insisted that he *either* accept the restrictions on his use of the car *or* not drive at all. *Neither* the manager *nor* the employee had a reasonable solution to the problem. *Whether* he stayed home *or* went to school depended on a change in his symptoms. *Both* the school board *and* the PTA agreed on the increase in funding for the new equipment. He was outstanding *not only* in his studies *but also* in sports.

Sentence Organization within Paragraphs

- A paragraph presents a larger unit of thought than a sentence can contain. A paragraph must meet certain requirements:

- A paragraph should have *unity,* that is, internal consistency. It should not digress from the dominant idea expressed in the topic sentence.

- A paragraph should have *completeness.* It should present enough detailed information about the topic sentence to answer any general questions the reader may have. More specific questions would require additional paragraphs with new topic sentences.

- A paragraph should have *coherence.* Sentences should flow into each other so that the reader experiences the paragraph as an integrated unit, not as a collection of separate sentences.

- A paragraph should have *order*. Like structure in a larger work, order in a paragraph grows partly out of the material and is partly imposed by the writer. Most paragraphs and essays follow one of the two patterns that follow.

    -- *From the general to the particular:* This type of paragraph begins with a topic sentence that serves as an introductory summary of the topic. The remaining sentences explain or illustrate this statement, so that the idea becomes increasingly clear as the paragraph progresses. The topic sentence is usually at or near the beginning of the paragraph.

    -- *From the particular to the general:* This type of paragraph is the reverse of the previous pattern. It begins with a series of explanatory or illustrative statements that lead to a general statement or summary. The topic sentence is usually at or near the end of the paragraph. A paragraph can be looked upon as a microcosm, an exact parallel in miniature of the entire work:

- It has a dominant idea, usually expressed in a topic sentence.

- The dominant idea is developed by examples, comparisons, explanations, or arguments to make the meaning of the topic sentence clear.

- There is usually a concluding restatement of the topic idea, a final sentence that parallels the concluding paragraph of an essay.

Capitalization

Definition: Capitalization is the use of capital letters to place special emphasis on particular letters to set them off from lower-case letters.

- Sentences always begin with a capital letter.

- The first letter of a quotation is always capitalized.

- Proper nouns, that is, nouns that name particular persons, places, or things must be capitalized. **Examples:** Appalachian Mountains, Mississippi River, Brooklyn Bridge

- Titles that precede a proper name are capitalized; those that follow a proper name are not. Examples: Chairperson John Smith and John Smith, the chairperson

Punctuation

Definition: Punctuation is the use of periods, commas, semicolons, colons, question marks, exclamation points, dashes, apostrophes, brackets, parentheses, slashes, and quotation marks to convey the pauses and gestures that we use in speech to clarify and emphasize meaning.

- Use a period to end a sentence. **Example:** She went to the beach.

- Use a period after abbreviations. **Examples:** Mr. Ms. U.S. Corp.

- Use a comma to separate independent clauses in a compound sentence. **Example:** Suzanne made a presentation at the conference, and then she spent the remainder of the day touring the city. Restrictive dependent clauses are not required to be set off by commas. **Example:** That *he would survive* is doubtful.

- Use a comma to separate an introductory phrase or clause from the main clause of a sentence. **Example:** After completing the work, the contractor left the site.
- Place a comma after every item in a series. **Example:** The new office is furnished with a desk, a computer, two chairs, and a supply cabinet.

- Two or more adjectives that modify the noun that they precede are separated by commas. **Example:** The cold, windy morning was not a good beginning for their vacation.

- An appositive is a word or group of words that renames or identifies a noun or pronoun that it follows. Nonrestrictive appositives--those that are not essential to the meaning of a sentence--are set off by commas. **Example:** Ken Fowler, the orthopedic surgeon, was appointed Chief of Staff. Restrictive appositives--those that are essential to the meaning of the sentence--are not set off by commas. **Example:** The author Stephen King is known for his frightening stories.

- Commas are used to set off the items in a date. **Example:** Monday, August 17, 2003, he became the head of the office. Commas are not used when only the month and year are given. Example: August 2003

- A semicolon is used to separate elements in a series when some of the elements already contain commas. **Example:** Sally wishes that we attend the first, third, and fifth sessions on Wednesday; the second, fourth, and sixth sessions on Thursday; and the first only on Friday.

- Periods and commas at the end of a quote always go inside quotation marks. **Example:** Georgia said, "I do not wish to receive the award solely for the work I did on that particular project."

- Punctuation marks other than periods or commas should be placed inside the quotation marks only when they apply to the matter quoted. **Example:** As mentioned by our new director, what do you think is the "acceptable method of producing exemplary behavior"?

Spelling

- Distinguish between ie and ei. Remember that it is i before e except after c and, also, when the vowel sound in the word has the long a sound.

Examples:

i before *e*	*e* before *i* after *c*	*e* before *i* when sounded like a long *a*
believe	ceiling	sleigh
relief	deceive	weigh
shield	receive	vein

- Drop the final *e* before adding a suffix that begins with a vowel. Keep the final *e* before adding a suffix that begins with a consonant. Examples:

drive	driving	sure	surely
chime	chiming	entire	entirety
become	becoming	like	likeness
age	aging	force	forceful

Exceptions:
dye   dyeing (to distinguish from *die*   *dying*)

Final *e* remains to keep the soft *c* or *g* sound before a suffix beginning with *a* or *i*.

change	changeable
notice	noticeable
singe	singeing However, *practice* becomes *practicable* because the soft *c* changes to the hard *k* sound.)

Some words that take *ful* or *ly* drop the final *e*.

true	truly
due	duly
awe	awful

- A word ending in y changes the y to *i* before adding a suffix beginning with *i*. **Examples:**

forty	fortieth
rectify	rectifier
defy	defiance (However, *cry* becomes *crying* not *criing*.)

- The final consonant is doubled before adding a suffix beginning with a vowel only when the following two criteria are met:
  1) a single vowel precedes the consonant, and
  2) the consonant ends a one-syllable word an accented syllable.

  Examples:

pop	popping
drop	dropping
rip	ripping
begin	beginning

- Nouns ending in a sound that can be smoothly united with s form their plurals by adding s. **Examples:**

Singular	*Plural*
cup	cups
pencil	pencils
folder	folders
frame	frames
boat	boats

- Nouns ending in a sound that cannot be smoothly united with *s* form their plurals by adding *es*. **Examples:**

Singular	Plural
fox	foxes
pass	passes
church	churches

- Nouns ending in y preceded by a consonant form their plurals by changing y to *i* and adding es. The exceptions are proper nouns ending in y. They simply add an *s* without dropping the y. **Examples:**

Singular	Plural
lady	ladies
fly	flies
ruby	rubies
body	bodies

Exception: There are two Henrys assigned to my project.

- Nouns ending in y preceded by *a, e, o,* or *u* form their plurals by only adding an *s*. **Examples:**

Singular	Plural
bay	bays
key	keys
toy	toys
guy	guys

- Plural nouns taken from other languages retain their foreign plural spelling. **Examples:**

Singular	Plural
datum	data
thesis	theses
phenomenon	phenomena
alumna (fem.)	alumnae
alumnus (mas.)	alumni

- Some foreign words keep their foreign plural and an anglicized one. Both are correct. **Examples:**

Singular	Plural (foreign)	Plural (anglicized)
focus	foci	focuses
memorandum	memoranda	memorandums
radius	radii	radiuses
index	indices	indexes
appendix	appendices	appendixes

- Use a hyphen to join two or more words serving as a single adjective before a noun. But, never hyphenate the same adjectives when following the verb. Example:

a well-equipped van	no hyphen for ... The van was well equipped.
a garish-red cloak	no hyphen for ... The cloak was garish red.
the well-read scholar	no hyphen for ... The scholar was well read.

The exception is when the first word is an adverb ending in *ly*. In that case, omit the hyphen.

Examples:

      a quick-moving river   or   a quickly moving river
      a swift-running competitor   or   a swiftly running competitor

- Hyphens should be used to avoid an ambiguous or awkward union of letters. **Examples:**

  re-enter, pre-election, pre-eminence, re-address
  Exceptions: cooperation, coeducational, zoology

- Hyphens are used to form all compound numbers between twenty-one and ninety-nine, and to separate the numerator from the denominator when fractions are written.
Examples:

  thirty-three, sixty-five, one-third, two-fourths

- Always use a hyphen with the prefixes *ex, self,* and all and the suffix *elect*. **Examples:**
  all-American, self-composed, ex-wife, president-elect
  Note: Do not capitalize *ex* or *elect* even when used in titles. **Examples:**
  ex-Governor Riley, Mayor-elect Johnson

BASIC FUNDAMENTALS OF ENGLISH EXPRESSION

TABLE OF CONTENTS

		Page
A.	FUNCTIONAL INTRODUCTION TO GRAMMAR	1
	<u>Classification</u>	1
	1. Nominative Absolute … 21. Verbals	1
	<u>Syntax</u>	1
	I. Uses of the Noun	1
	II. Uses of the Pronoun	2
	III. Uses of the Adjective	4
	IV. Uses of the Adverb	4
	V. Uses of Verbals	4
	VI. Uses of Phrases	5
	VII. Uses of Subordinate Clauses	6
	VIII. Uses of the Verb	6
	IX. Special Uses	7
B.	BASIC SYNTAX	8
	Rules 1-9	8
	Rules 10-21	9
	Rules 22-34	10
	Rules 35-38	11
C.	COMMON ERRORS IN USAGE	11

BASIC FUNDAMENTALS OF ENGLISH EXPRESSION

A. FUNCTIONAL INTRODUCTION TO GRAMMAR

For examination purposes, there are two clear-cut and yet related divisions in grammar: classification and syntax.

Classification refers to the required nomenclature for the proper identification and description of the uses of words or groups of words. Syntax refers to the relations of words and groups of words with one another in sentences.

The more usual terms of Classification are the following:

CLASSIFICATION

1. Nominative Absolute
2. Nominative of Direct Address
3. Nominative of Exclamation
4. Predicate Nominative
5. Predicate Adjective
6. Object of a Verb
7. Indirect Object
8. Object of a Preposition
9. Objective Complement
10. Adverbial Objective
11. Retained Object
12. Noun in Apposition
13. Auxiliary Verb
14. Copulative Verb
15. Progressive Forms of the Verb
16. Past Participle
17. Mood
18. Tense
19. Subject - complete subject, including modifiers
20. Predicate - verb and all modifiers and complements
21. Verbals

The more outstanding and the more frequently occurring types of syntactical relationships are defined in the illustrations appearing hereafter.

SYNTAX

I. Uses of the Noun
    A. Nominative Case:
        1. Subject of a verb: MARY bought a hat.
        2. Predicate Nominative: (Double Function)
            a. With a copulative verb: He became PRESIDENT. Is that the SORT of a person you take me for?
            b. With a verb in the passive voice: He was chosen PRESIDENT.
        3. Independent Constructions:
            a. Noun in Apposition with a noun in the nominative case: My sister, CLARA, is going with me.
            b. Nominative Absolute: The TRAIN having stopped, the passengers got out. James stood before me, his HANDS in his pocket
            c. Nominative of Direct Address: MARY, open the door.
            d. Nominative of Exclamation: What a MAN!

B. Possessive Case:
   1. To show ownership: MARY'S hat is brown.
   2. To indicate the relation of the doer to an act expressed in a particular noun: MARY'S having her homework saved the day. (See Predicate Complement of Copulative Verbal, below)
C. Objective Case: (Complements)
   1. Object of a
      a. Verb: The child ate the APPLE.
      b. Verbal:
         1. Infinitive: At times, it's a pleasure to eat an APPLE.
         2. Participle: Having lost the larger PART of his fortune, my friend found that economy was necessary.
         3. Participial Noun: Eating an APPLE is a pleasure.
      c. Preposition: She gave the book to CLARA.
      d. Cognate Object: He spoke his SPEECH well.
      e. Secondary Object of a Verb or Verbal: He told John the ANSWER. He asked John a QUESTION. He paid his workers good WAGES. (Differs from the indirect object because the secondary object can be dropped.)
   2. Indirect Object of a
      a. Verb: We gave JOHN our books.
      b. Verbal:
         1. Infinitive: He asked us to give CATHERINE the money.
         2. Participle: Giving my FRIEND the money I had borrowed, I heaved a sigh of relief.
         3. Participial Noun: Giving PEOPLE money makes most people happier.
   3. Subject of an Infinitive: I expect JOHN to be present. Let ME rest!
   4. Objective Complement: (See Predicate Nominative with Passive Verb) We elected him PRESIDENT. The Romans called Caesar FRIEND.
   5. Retained Object:(See 2a.)John was given our BOOKS.
   6. Adverbial Objective: I wanted to go HOME. The child is three YEARS old.
   7. Predicate Complement of Copulative Verbals:
      a. Referring back to the Subject of the Infinitive: I believed Allen to be the MAN.
      b. Referring back to the noun modified by a participle:
         Or lonely house,
         Long held the witches' HOME.
      c. Referring back to the Possessive with the Participial Noun: There is sense in your hoping to be SECRETARY. I was sure of John's being the AGGRESSOR.
   8. Noun in Apposition with a noun in the objective case: I gave the song, SOPHISTICATED LADY, to my friend to play.

II. Uses of the Pronoun
   A. Personal Pronouns: Similar to nouns in use, but, in addition, they must agree with the antecedent in person, number, and gender.
      1. Nominative Case:
         a. Subject of a verb: SHE bought a hat.
         b. Predicate Nominative with Copulative Verb: It is I
         c. Independent Construction:
            1. Nominative Absolute: SHE being ill, we decided to go.

2. Nominative of Direct Address: YOU, will you come!
3. Nominative of Exclamation: I! You cannot accuse me!
   2. Possessive Case:
      a. To show ownership: HER hat is brown.
      b. To indicate relation of doer to an act or state expressed in a participial noun: HIS having a car saved the day.
   3. Objective Case:
      a. Object of a
         1. Verb: The child ate IT.
         2. Verbal:
            a. Infinitive: At times it is a pleasure to eat IT.
            b. Participle: Having lost IT, we hunted for another.
            c. Participial Noun: Taking IT in large doses is bad.
         3. Preposition: She referred me to HIM for an answer.
      b. Indirect Object of a
         1. Verb: We gave HIM our books.
         2. Verbal:
            a. Infinitive: He asked us to give HER the money.
            b. Participle: Giving HIM the money I had borrowed, I heaved a sigh of relief.
            c. Participial Noun: Giving HIM money made him unhappy.
      c. Subject of the Infinitive: I expected HIM to be present.
      d. Retained Object: He was given IT for his own use.
B. Uses of "it":
   1. Impersonal Pronoun, subject of a verb when no definite subject is expressed: IT rains.
   2. Expletive, serving to introduce the verb "is" when the real subject is in the Predicate: IT may be true that he did not commit the crime.
C. Compound Personal Pronouns:
   1. Intensively: I, MYSELF, will go.
   2. Reflexively: I have harmed MYSELF. The neighbors left us severely to OURSELVES.
D. Interrogative Pronouns: Similar to personal pronouns in use, but, in addition, they assist in asking a question. WHO is that? WHOSE is that? WHOM do you expect? WHICH is the better student? WHAT is your aim in life? He asked me WHAT I had meant by that statement.(Indirect) WHO do you consider is the best agent the company has?
E. Adjective (Demonstrative) Pronouns: Similar to personal pronouns in use. THIS is a new hat. THESE are very interesting books. The mountains of Colorado are higher than THOSE. I bought ONE, too.
F. Relative Pronouns: Similar to personal pronouns in use, but, in addition, they <u>connect</u> the adjective clauses they introduce with the nouns or pronouns modified.
   That is the girl WHO is going with me.
   The men WHOM you see there are marines.
   The men WHOSE lights are lit are seniors.
   Ask her for the book WHICH I recommended.
   Tell her WHAT you have told me. (That which)
   That's WHAT I did it for.
   The book THAT I gave her is lost.
   This is the pillow THAT I asked for.

Who do you consider is the best agent (THAT) the company has? (Elliptical use)

Adjective clauses are also introduced by relative adverbs:
There was one time WHEN I almost caught you.
That is the house WHERE I was born.

    G. Compound relative pronouns:
I will go with WHOEVER is going my way. (Implies own antecedent: HIM WHO)

III. Uses of the Adjective
    A. Modifier of a noun (pronoun): That was an ORIENTAL rug. This dress is plainer than that PRETTY one. I must have the test-tube CLEAN. Of dark BROWN gardens and of PEEPING flowers.
    B. Predicate Adjective:
        1. With copulative verb: She was LAZY. This apple is RIPE.
        2. Passive Voice: This man was pronounced GUILTY.
    C. Objective Complement: I called the ship UNSEAWORTHY. I will make assurance doubly SURE. She wiped the plate DRY.

IV. Uses of the Adverb
    A. Modifier of a verb: She walked RAPIDLY. This matter must be acted UPON.
    B. Modifier of a verbal:
        1. Infinitive: She attempted to walk RAPIDLY.
        2. Participle: Having arrived SILENTLY, she overheard the conversation.
        3. Participial Noun: Passing COMMENDABLY is our aim.
    C. Modifier of an adjective: The ice was UNUSUALLY smooth this winter.
    D. Modifier of another adverb: The wheels revolved VERY swiftly.
    E. Modifier of a phrase or clause: He arrived JUST in time. That is EXACTLY what I expected of him.
    F. As a relative or conjunctive adverb, introducing a clause and modifying the verb in this clause: I passed the house WHERE he was born. AS he rose from his chair, the audience burst into wild applause.
    G. As an interrogative adverb, asking a direct or indirect question and modifying the verb: WHEN did you arrive? Tell us WHY he is always successful.

V. Uses of Verbals: Verbals take adverbial modifiers and complements.
    A. The Infinitive.
        1. As a noun
            a. Nominative Case:
                1. Subject of Verb: TO EXIST is a hard job these days.
                2. Predicate Nominative: Copulative Verb: To work is TO EAT.
                3. Independent Constructions: Apposition: Our ambition, TO ACT, was never realized.
                4. Nominative Absolute: To ENJOY ourselves being impossible, we left the theatre.
                5. Exclamation: TO SOAR! TO SOAR above the earth with wings!
            b. Objective Case:
                1. Object of a verb: The child asked TO SING. They expect TO TAKE one.
                2. Object of a verbal:(Infinitive) It is never safe to ask TO GO. (Participle) Having asked TO LEAVE, he refused when the chance came. Bill Brown came asking
TO BE ADMITTED to the house. (Participial Noun) Learning TO FLY is amusing.

3. Object of a Preposition: There was nothing to do but TO GO.
4. Retained Object: He was told TO GO.
5. Apposition with noun in objective case: We never realized our ambition, TO ACT.
6. Special Use: With an object noun or pronoun as its subject: I wrote for him TO COME.(Such phrases introduced by "for" are used as nouns.) He felt the ground TREMBLE.

2. As an adjective
   a. Modifying a noun: Houses TO RENT are scarce this year.
   c. Predicate Adjective: Our plan seemed TO WORK each day.
3. As an adverb
   a. Modifying a verb: Folks would laugh TO SEE a cindermaid at a court ball.
   b. Modifying an adjective: The army was ready TO MARCH.
   c. Modifying a verbal: (Participle) Having gone out TO SHOP, he could not be found. (Participial Noun) Trying TO STUDY is impossible.
4. As part of the complement of a verb or preposition with a noun as subject: Let me GO!
5. As an Independent Expression: TO LIVE! To live in utter forgetfulness.

B. The Participle: The participial form of a verb used as an adjective: The men HAVING WORKED steadily, the company decided to give them a raise. (Predicate Adjective) He appeared PANTING. (Objective Complement) I must have the test-tube CLEANED. Special Case: (1) With a noun in the nominative absolute construction: The day HAVING DAWNED, we started on our trip. (2) In rare cases, as an adverb: He ran CRYING down the street.

C. The Participal Noun: The participial form of a verb used as a noun. (Subject) SEEING is believing. (Predicate Nominative)Seeing is BELIEVING. (Apposition) The sport, SKATING, is an exciting one. (Nominative Absolute) SKATING being over, the children went home. (With Possessive Pronoun) MARY'S swimming did not succeed very well. (Object of verb) I love SKATING. (Object of Verbal) He wanted to go SKATING. (Object of a Preposition) The pleasure lies in EATING. We went SKATING. (Retained Object) The children were given WEAVING to do. (Adverbial Objective) That is worth THINKING about. The water was BOILING hot.

VI. Uses of Phrases
  A. As nouns:
   1. The Infinitive Phrase: His aim is TO BE WELL.
   2. Participial Noun Phrase: His only pleasure is BEING WELL. MENDING BROKEN CHINA was his occupation.
  B. As adjectives:
  1. Prepositional Phrase:(Modifier of a Noun) The trees OF THE FOREST are fading. (Predicate Adjective) The sun is IN ITS SPLENDOR.
  2. Infinitive Phrase: (Modifier of a Noun) The house TO BE SOLD was burned. (Predicate Adjective) The house was TO BE SOLD.
  3. Participial Phrase: (Modifier of Noun) RUNNING AWAY, he was shot.
  C. As adverbs:
   1. Prepositional Phrase: Frank came A-RUNNING. Tom ran crying DOWN THE STREET. The room was full OF PEOPLE.
   2. Infinitive Phrase: Folks would laugh TO SEE a cindermaid at a ball.
  D. As Independent Elements: It is true, TO BE SURE. It is better, IN MY OPINION, to face the situation directly.

VII. Uses of Subordinate Clauses
   A. Noun Clauses: Introduced by subordinating conjunctions such as THAT, WHETHER; interrogative pronouns in indirect questions, such as WHO, WHICH, WHAT; interrogative adverbs in indirect questions, such as WHERE, WHEN, WHY, HOW; all illustrated below.
      1. Subject of a Verb: THAT WE HAVE SURVIVED THE ORDEAL is evident.
      2. Predicate Nominative: The truth is THAT HE FAILED TO PASS.
      3. Noun in Apposition: The fact THAT THE EARTH IS ROUND is never disputed.
      4. Object of a Verb or Verbal: Tell me WHERE IS FANCY BRED. I wish HE WOULD HELP ME, I begged him to tell me WHAT HE WANTED. I asked him just WHAT HE REPORTED.
      5. Object of a Preposition: I am going there no matter WHAT YOU SAY. We came to the conclusion from WHAT WE KNOW.
      6. Retained Object: He was asked just WHAT HE REPORTED. I was asked WHETHER I ENJOY READING.
      7. Special Construction: In apposition with the expletive IT: It is commonly known THAT HE CANNOT BE TRUSTED.
   B. Adjective Clauses: Introduced by relative pronoun, WHO, WHICH, WHAT, THAT; relative adverb, WHERE, WHEN, AFTER.
      1. Modifier of a Noun: Thrice is he armed WHO HATH HIS QUARREL JUST. There is society WHERE NONE INTRUDES. I remember the house WHERE I WAS BORN. Who do you consider is the best agent THE COMPANY HAS?
   C. Adverbial Clauses: Introduced by relative (or conjunctive) adverbs; subordinating conjunctions such as BECAUSE, IF, SINCE, THOUGH.
      1. Modifier of a Verb, Verbal, Adjective, Adverb: Try AS WE MAY, we cannot swim to that rock. I intend to leave WHEN YOU GO. We are glad THAT YOU ARE WITH US. WHERE THE BEE SUCKS, there suck I.
   D. Independent Clause Element: Who DO YOU CONSIDER is the best agent the company has? He is, I THINK, able to do the work well.
VIII. Uses of the Verb
   A. Types of verbs
      1. Transitive verbs
         a. These require direct objects to complete the meaning: John ATE the apple, (direct object)
      2. Intransitive verbs
         a. These do not require an object to complete the meaning: The boy RAN down the mountain. (Common causes of error are the misuse of the intransitive verbs RISE, LIE, and SIT and/or the transitive verbs RAISE, LAY, and SET: She LAID on the bed, for She LAY on the bed.
      3. Copulative verbs
         a. These verbs, especially forms of the verb TO BE, are used to express simply the relationship between the subject and the predicate (or complement): She LOOKS good; The meat SMELLS bad; I FEEL better. (The most common copulative verbs are: BE, SEEM, PROVE, FEEL, SOUND, LOOK, APPEAR, BECOME, TASTE.)
      4. Auxiliary verbs
         a. These verbs assist in forming the voices, modes, and tenses of other verbs: She SHOULD go; They HAVE BEEN gone a month; We WERE given the information. (The most common auxiliary verbs are: BE,

HAVE, DO, SHALL, WILL, MAY, CAN, MUST, OUGHT, with all their inflectional forms.)
- B. Tenses of verbs (Verbs appear in different forms to indicate the time of the action):
  1. Present tense: The boy CARRIES the book; She EATS cookies.
  2. Past tense: The men COMPLETED the job; We VISITED him at home.
  3. Future tense: We WILL DO the job tomorrow; I SHALL GO alone.
     - a. In speech and in informal writing, WILL and WOULD are now commonly used for all three persons except for the use of SHOULD to express obligation.
     - b. In formal writing and careful usage, the following distinctions are observed between SHALL and WILL:
       1. To express simple futurity, use SHALL (or SHOULD) with the first person, and WILL (or WOULD) with the second or third persons: I SHALL be glad to go; They WOULD like to go.
       2. To express determination, intention, etc., use WILL (or WOULD) with the first person, and SHALL (or SHOULD) with the second and third persons: I WILL do it; You SHALL not go; They SHALL not pass.
       3. In questions, use SHALL with the first person: SHALL we see you tonight? SHALL I do it now? With the second person, use the form that is expected in the answer: WILL you lend us the car? (The answer that is expected here is: I WILL or I WILL not.) With the third person, use WILL to express simple futurity: WILL there be someone to meet him at the train?
       4. In indirect discourse, use the auxiliary that would be used if the discourse were direct: The company asked him whether he WOULD pay the bill. (Direct discourse: WILL you pay the bill?) He stated that he WOULD undertake the mission. (Direct discourse: I WILL undertake the mission.) His wife asked him whether he SHOULD be late for supper. (Direct discourse: SHALL you be late for supper?)
  4. Present perfect tense: I HAVE BEEN LIVING here for three years.
  5. Past perfect tense: He HAD BEEN CONVICTED of a crime many years ago.
  6. Future perfect tense: Before you arrive, I SHALL HAVE BAKED the pie.
- C. Mood (Mode) (The forms of a verb that indiqate the manner of the action):
  1. Indicative Mood (used to state a fact or to ask a question): The man FELL; ARE you well?
  2. Imperative Mood (used to express a command or an urgent request): DO it at once; ANSWER the telephone.
  3. Subjective Mood (used to express a wish, a supposition, a doubt, an exhortation, a concession, a condition contrary to fact): Wish: If only I WERE able to run faster!
  Supposition: They will be married provided their parents CONSENT. Condition contrary to fact: If you HAD more experience, you would know how to handle the problem.

IX. Special Uses
- A. Common Words Used as Different Parts of Speech:
  1. But: as relative pronoun: There is none BUT will answer.
     as adverb: You are BUT half awake, (only)
     as a preposition: Every man BUT him may leave, (except)
     I cannot BUT feel cherful.(except to feel)

as a coordinating conjunction: He leaves BUT I stay.
2. Like: (Never used as a conjunction)
as a preposition: He talks LIKE his mother,
as a verb: I LIKE his manner of speech.
3. As: as a relative pronoun: You own the same AS I.
as an adverb: I am AS young as you are.
as a subordinating conjunction: I am as young AS you are.
as a preposition: He has frequently appeared AS Hamlet.
4. Than: as a preposition: He loves money more THAN learning.
as a subordinating conjunction: He knows more THAN I.

B. BASIC SYNTAX
(NOTE: Rules are numbered for reference.)
A <u>noun</u> is the name of a person, place, object, or Idea.
A <u>pronoun</u> is a word used in place of a noun.
Nouns and pronouns are called .substantives.
1. The subject of a verb is in the <u>nominative</u> case.
The <u>boy</u> threw the ball.
Transitive verbs express action upon an object or product.
2. The direct object of a transitive verb is in the <u>objective (accusative)</u> case. <u>Whom</u> shall I fear?
Intransitive verbs are often followed by substantives which rename their subject. Such complements are called <u>predicate nominatives</u>, <u>predicate nouns,</u> or <u>attribute complements.</u>
3. A substantive used as attribute complement agrees in case with the subject to which it refers.
It is <u>I</u>. <u>Whom</u> do you take me to be?
A substantive which helps to complete a verb but renames the object of the verb is called an <u>objective comp1ement.</u>
4. An <u>objective complement</u> is in the <u>objective</u> case.
The class elected him <u>president.</u>
5. The <u>object of a preposition</u> is in the <u>objective case.</u>
Give it to me. The cat is under the <u>stove.</u>
The receiver of an action may sometimes be thought of as the principal word in an adverbial phrase from which the preposition <u>to</u> or <u>for</u> is omitted. Such a complement is called an <u>indirect object.</u>
6. An <u>indirect object</u> is in the objective case (dative object). Bring <u>me</u> a chair.
<u>Infinitives</u> and <u>participles</u> do not really assert action or being, but they imply it, and in this sense may have subjects.
Verbs of wishing, desiring, commanding, believing, declaring, perceiving, etc., are likely to be followed by objects which are at the same time <u>subjects of verbals.</u> It is this objective relation which justifies Rule 7.
7. The subject of a verbal is in the objective case.(Except in independent phrases.)
She has <u>me</u> to protect her. We thought <u>him</u> to be honest.
8. Substantives used with verbals in independent phrases are in the nominative case. ("Absolute.")
His <u>friends</u> advising it, he resigned.
An appositive is a noun or pronoun used as explanatory of or equivalent to another noun or pronoun.
9. An appositive takes the case of the substantive to which it is attached.
The book was his, <u>Peter's.</u> (Possessive.)
'Tis I, Hamlet, the Dane. (Nominative.)

Give it to me your brother.(Objective.)

10. A noun or pronoun <u>independent by address</u> is in the <u>nominative</u> case. ("Vocative".)
    "<u>Hens of Athens.</u> Him declare I unto you."
    <u>Mr. President,</u> I rise to a point of order.

11. A noun or pronoun used <u>independently with a following adjective, adverb, or phrase</u> may best be regarded as in the objective case, since it is virtually the object in a prepositional phrase from which the preposition is omitted.
    <u>Hat in hand,</u> he stood waiting
    <u>Beard unkempt, clothes threadbare,</u> he looked down and out.
    <u>Fences down, weeds everywhere,</u> the place was desolate.

12. Nouns or pronouns showing ownership are in the <u>possessive</u> case.
    <u>John's</u> farm; <u>your</u> shoes.

13. When an inanimate thing is personified, the <u>gender</u> of its noun or pronoun is determied by custom.
    <u>She's</u> a good old boat! (Feminine.)
    The <u>sun</u> is hiding <u>his</u> head. (Masculine.)

14. <u>Collective nouns are plural</u> when their units act separately as individuals; <u>singular</u> when the units act together as one. <u>Plural titles</u> are in this sense singular nouns.
    The class has had its picture taken. (All together.)
    The class have had their pictures taken. (Each person by himself.)
    "The Newcomes" is by Thackeray.

15. <u>Nouns used adverbially</u> to measure time or distance are in the <u>objective case.</u> <u>(Adverbial objective.)</u>
    We walked an <u>hour</u>, travelled four <u>miles</u>.

16. A <u>substantive</u> used as an exclamation is commonly held to be <u>nominative.</u> But if the exclamation repeats an idea already used, it will take the case of the term repeated.
    We shall be rich. We! think of that!
    "We'll make you do it!" <u>Me!</u> I guess not!

17. A <u>pronoun</u> must agree with its antecedent in <u>number</u>, <u>gender</u>. and <u>person</u>. Collective nouns take singular pronouns when the units act separately
    The Ship of State has refused to obey <u>her</u> rudder.
    <u>That</u> is <u>he whom</u> you seek. (All three are in 3rd Person, Masculine Gender, Singular Number.)
    The <u>case</u> of a pronoun does not depend upon its antecedent, but upon its use in the sentence.
    A verb is a word which asserts. (Tells something of its subject.)

18. A verb agrees with its subject in person and number. *I* am: You <u>are</u>; He <u>is</u>; She goes; They <u>go</u> .

19. A compound subject with <u>and</u> takes a singular verb if the idea of the combined subject is of <u>one</u> thing; if the compound subject is made of parts acting separately, the verb is <u>plural.</u>
    Roosevelt and Wilson <u>were</u> of opposing parties.
    The sum and substance of the matter <u>is</u> this.

20. A <u>distributive</u> subject with each, <u>every, everyone, either, neither</u>. etc., requires a verb in the <u>singular</u>; a disjunctive subject with <u>either-or. neither-nor,</u> takes a verb in the <u>singular</u> if the substantives are singular.
    <u>Either</u> the book or the teacher <u>is</u> wrong.
    <u>Each</u> of us must use his own judgment.

21. <u>Nouns plural in form</u> but singular in meaning commonly take a verb in the <u>singular.</u>
    Hydraulics <u>is</u> a practical study nowadays.

Mumps <u>is</u> contagious.
The news <u>is</u> discouraging.

22. When the subject acts upon an object, the verb is in the <u>active voice;</u> when the subject is a receiver or product of action, the verb is <u>passive.</u>
The hunter <u>shot</u> the door. (Active.)
The deer <u>was shot</u> by the hunter. (Passive.)

23. The <u>indicative mood</u> is used in questions and in simple assertions of factor matter thought of as possible fact.
<u>Were</u> you there?
You <u>were</u> there.
If you <u>were</u> there, I did not see you.(See subjunctive mood, Rule 24.)

24. The <u>subjunctive mood</u> expresses a wish, or a <u>condition contrary to fact.</u>
Would he <u>were</u> here!
If he <u>were</u> here, we would know about it.
(Implying denial. He has.not been here.)

25. The <u>imperative mood</u> states a command or request. Please_go at once.
The subject of an imperative verb is you understood; the <u>you</u> is seldom expressed, unless the mood is emphatic.

26. <u>Infinitives</u> may be used as <u>subject, object of verb, attribute complement, object of preposition, appositive, adjective modifier,</u> adverbial modifier, or in an <u>independent phrase.</u>
For examples, see discussion of <u>Verbals</u> in this section.

27. <u>Gerunds</u> (Verbal nouns in ing) have the uses of <u>nouns</u> together with the power of implying action, being or condition.
Examples have been given under <u>uses</u> of Verbals.

28. <u>Participles</u> may be used as <u>adjectives,</u> adverbs, <u>subjective complements, objective complements, following a preposition,</u> or in <u>absolute phrases.</u>
See examples under Verbals.

29. The comparative degree of adjectives and adverbs, not the superlative degree, is used in comparing two persons or things.
He is the <u>taller</u> of the two; in fact, the <u>tallest</u> of the three.

30. A <u>coordinating conjunction</u> connects words, phrases, or clauses of like rank, grammatically independent of each other.
I will come if I can <u>and</u> if the weather is good.

31. A <u>subordinating conjunction</u> joins a dependent clause to a principal one.
Make hay <u>while</u> the sun shines.

32. <u>Interjections</u> commonly have no grammatical relation in the sentence. In certain constructions, however, the interjection seems to have a phrasal modifier.
"Ah! for the pirate's dream of fight!"

33. Verbs <u>become, feel, look,</u> see, <u>smell, taste, sound, grow</u> may take an <u>attribute complement</u> to describe the subject, or an adverb to modify the assertion of the verb.
He grew <u>tall.</u> Poisonous mushrooms taste <u>good.</u>
"He looks <u>well</u>" may describe his own condition, and so the word <u>well</u> may be a predicate adjective relating to the subject; or the sentence may mean that he <u>searches thoroughly.</u> in which sense <u>well</u> is an adverb modifying <u>looks.</u>

34. <u>Assertions of Simple Futurity</u> take the form
    I, we   shall
    You   will
    He, they   will

<u>Assertions of Strong Purpose, Promise, Threat, Consent</u> take the form I, we will You shall He, they shall

35. Adjectives should not take the place of adverbs, nor adverbs the place of adjectives.

36. The six tenses of English verbs in the Active Voice, Indicative Mood, are built up from the "principal parts" as follows:

Present Tense, Past Tense, as in Principal Parts, Future Tense, <u>shall</u> or will (Rule 34) with Present Infinitive (less "to").

Present Perfect, <u>have</u> or has. with Past Participle Past Perfect, <u>had,</u> with Past Participle.
Future Perfect, <u>shall</u> or <u>will</u> (Rule 34), with Present Perfect, the "have" form.

37. The six tenses of English verbs in the Passive Voice, Indicative Mood, invariably use the past participle of the given verb, preceded by an appropriate form of the verb "be."

38. <u>Gerunds,</u> being verbal nouns, are modified by adjectives and <u>possessive pronouns.</u>

Now do it without <u>my</u> watching you.

C. COMMON ERRORS IN USAGE

(Numbers refer to rules in the preceding section. Correct forms are given first.)

	RULE
This is the <u>better</u> of the two. *NOT* this is the <u>best</u> of the two	(29)
<u>You</u> and I, did it. *NOT* <u>you</u> and <u>me</u> did it, *NOR* <u>me</u> and <u>you</u>.	(1)
<u>We</u> boys will be there. *NOT* <u>us</u> boys will be there.	(1)
It was <u>I, she, he, they</u>. *NOT* <u>me, her, him, them</u>.	(3)
We believed it to be <u>her, him, them</u>. *NOT* <u>she, he, they</u>.	(3)
Between you and <u>me</u>. *NOT* between you and <u>I.</u>	(5)
She is taller than <u>I,</u> (am). *NOT* she is taller than <u>me.</u>	(1)
It was known to be <u>he</u>. *NOT* <u>him</u>. He agrees with "It."	(3)
We were sure of its being <u>him</u>. (Usage divided.)	(3,5)
Let everybody bring <u>his own</u> lunch. *NOT* <u>their own</u>.	(14,17,24)
We should all bring <u>our</u> lunches.(Action concerted.)	(17)
Every boy and girl should do his best. <u>Their</u> would be incorrect.	
<u>His</u> or <u>her</u> is correct, for formal,	(17)
Each of us <u>has his</u> problems. *NOT* <u>have their.</u>	(20)
The actor <u>whom</u> you saw was Otis Skinner. *NOT* <u>who.</u>	(2)
<u>Whom</u> did you call for? *NOT* <u>who.</u>	(5)
<u>Whom</u> did you select? *NOT* <u>who.</u>	(2)
<u>Who</u> do you suppose it is? <u>Who</u> agrees with <u>it.</u>	(3)
<u>Who</u> do you think I am? *NOT* <u>whom</u>. Agrees with <u>I.</u>	(3)
<u>Whom</u> did you take me to be? <u>Whom</u> agrees with <u>me.</u>	(3)
The tree looks <u>beautiful</u>. *NOT* beautifully.	(33)
The apple tastes <u>good.</u> *NOT* <u>well.</u>	(33)
The tune sounds <u>harsh.</u>	(33)
Roses smell <u>sweet.</u> *NOT* <u>sweetly.</u>	(33)
She looks <u>charming</u>. *NOT* <u>charmingly.</u>	(33)
We <u>shall</u> be drowned if we go there. NOT <u>we will be</u>	(34)
I <u>shall</u> be pleased to help you. *NOT* <u>will</u> be.	(34)
The senate has adjourned. *NOT* <u>have</u> adjourned.	(14)
There <u>are</u> all sorts of graft in town. *NOT* there <u>is</u> all sorts.	(18)
Here <u>are</u> wealth and beauty. *NOT* here <u>is</u>. (Unless taken separately.)	(18)
Neither of the men shows signs of giving *in*. *NOT* neither show.	(18)
In both cases, there <u>are</u> bad birth and misfortune. *NOT* there is. (Unless taken separately.)	(18)
Our class poet <u>believes</u> in symbolism. *NOT* <u>believe.</u>	(18)

He is one of the best actors that have ever been here. NOT has. (17,18)
Let him who will, come. NOT let he. (2)
The congregation were free to express their opinions, OR was free to
  express its opinions. (14)
I saw. NOT I seen. (36)
I did. NOT I done. (36)
We have gone. NOT have went. (36)
We were. NOT we was. (18)
You began it. NOT you begun it. (36)
The wind blew. NOT the wind blowed. (36)
The glass is broken. NOT broke. (37)
I caught, have caught. NOT catched, have catched. (36)
Have been chosen. NOT have been chose. (37)
We came along. NOT we come. (36)
We have come. NOT have came. (36)
The-baby crept. NOT creeped. (36)
You've done it. NOT you've did it. (36)
We drew. NOT we drawed. (36)
He has drunk a glassful. NOT has drank (36)
Have driven. NOT have drove. (36)
Have eaten. NOT have ate. (36)
I ate my dinner. NOT eat (36)
Eas fallen. NOT has fell. (36)
The boys fought. NOT fit. (36)
Has flown, NOT has flew. (36)
I've forgotten. NOT forgot. (36)
It grew. NOT it growed. (36)
You lie low. NOT lay low. (Lie, to recline; lay, to put down.) (36)
Have ridden. NOT have rode. (36)
We rang the bell. NOT we rung it. (36)
Had risen. NOT had rose. (36)
And then I ran away. NOT then I run away. (36)
Ve sang a song. NOT we sung it. (36)
Troubles sprang up. NOT troubles sprung up. (36)
Somebody has stolen my hat. NOT has stole. (36)
The place stunk. NOT stank. (36)
We swam a mile. NOT we swum. (36)
Who's taken my hat? NOT who's took? (36)
Have torn. .NOT have tore. (36)
Have written. NOT have wrote. (36)
Say it slowly. NOT slow. (35)
We can do that as easily as you please. NOT as easy. (35)
The horse threw my brother and me out. NOT my brother and I. (2)
We chose the foreman who we thought could handle the men. NOW whom. (1)
I never saw a taller man than he. NOT him. (1)
There isn't another girl in town so handsome as she. NOT her. (1)
MOSSES FROM AN OLD MANSE is a collection of essays and stories.
  NOT are a collection. (14)
Now skate without my helping you. NOT me helping. (38)
We ought to keep still about his being here. NOT him being. (38)

www.ingramcontent.com/pod-product-compliance
Lightning Source LLC
Chambersburg PA
CBHW082122230426
43671CB00015B/2779